975.6

Kup
pb

ROANOKE

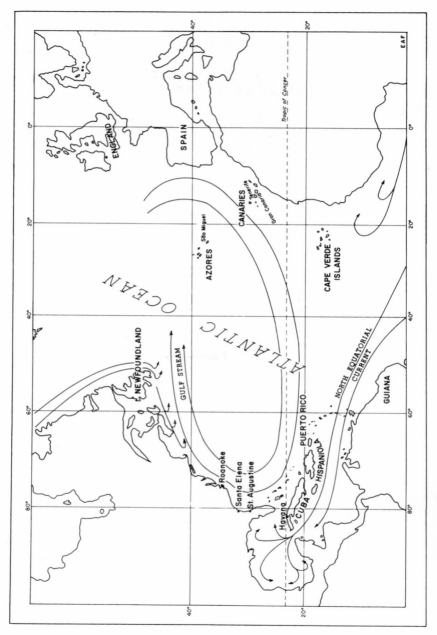

Figure 1.   The Atlantic Ocean

ROANOKE
THE ABANDONED COLONY

Karen Ordahl Kupperman

Rowman & Littlefield Publishers, Inc.

For my parents
Grace Swanson Ordahl and Stafford Newell Ordahl

The map of Virginia on the cover is reproduced by permission of the trustees of the British Museum and the University of North Carolina Press.

The maps of the Atlantic Basin (frontispiece) and the Indian Jurisdictions, 1585, (following page 74) were produced by the University of Connecticut Cartography Lab. The latter is after a map based on data from Christian F. Feest in Handbook of North American Indians, Volume 15, *Northeast*, ed. Bruce G. Trigger. The series is under the general editorship of William C. Sturtevant.

ROWMAN & LITTLEFIELD PUBLISHERS, INC.

Published in the United States of America
by Rowman & Littlefield Publishers, Inc.
8705 Bollman Place, Savage, Maryland 20763

Copyright © 1984 by Rowman & Allanheld

British Cataloging in Publication Information Available

Library of Congress Cataloging-in-Publication Data

Kupperman, Karen Ordahl, 1939-
  Roanoke, the abandoned colony.
  1. Raleigh's Roanoke colonies, 1584-1590.   2. Roanoke Island (N.C.)-
History.   3. Algonquian Indians-First contact with Occidental
civilization.   4. Indians of North America-North Carolina-First contact
with Occidental civilization.
  I. Title.
F229.K9 1984
975.6'175   83-24419 CIP

ISBN 0-8476-7339-1 (pbk. : alk. paper)

Printed in the United States of America

TABLE OF CONTENTS

PREFACE

ROANOKE is a twice-forgotten colony. It was abandoned by its sixteenth-century founders and has been almost completely ignored by twentieth-century Americans. Few today know the heroic and tragic story of the small group of English men and women who founded the first English colony in North America. I originally decided to write this book because whenever I tell people that I work on the earliest colonies, they invariably reply, "Oh, you mean the Pilgrims." Almost the first half-century of American history is gone from the popular consciousness. This is doubly wrong: Americans should understand the magnitude of the effort invested by both Indians and Europeans in the founding of this nation; they are also cheating themselves of one of the most dramatic and interesting stories in our history.

It is possible to write Roanoke's story in depth because a sixteenth-century Englishman, Richard Hakluyt, who believed England's future greatness would come through world trade and overseas colonies, decided to collect and publish every narrative, reminiscence, and letter from those involved in exploration and colonization. He accomplished his goal so well that we can know the Roanoke colonists and their backers more intimately than historical figures much closer to us in time. Hakluyt's modern counterpart, whose contribution is no less valuable, is Professor David B. Quinn. His work on sixteenth-century colonization and exploration is unparalleled. Professor Quinn has put together all the documents connected with Roanoke, those published originally by Hakluyt as well as sources later discovered in English and Spanish archives, in a two-volume collection, *The Roanoke Voyages, 1584–1590* (London, 1955). Anyone who wants to explore further in this subject and to hear the colonists tell their own stories should dip into these volumes; all quotes from the colonists in this book can be found there. The excellent notes provide a sure guide through the thickets of sixteenth-century prose style. David and Alison Quinn

have graciously shared knowledge, speculations, and hunches with me.
I am grateful for their friendship.

Many readers will want to go to the Outer Banks themselves and see
the site of these adventures. The staff at the Fort Raleigh National
Historic Site is impressive; Phillip Evans was particularly helpful to
me. Americans should take advantage of the excellent nation-wide system of historic sites run by knowledgeable National Park Service
rangers. Fort Raleigh, with its reconstructed earthen fort, is an excellent introduction not only to Roanoke but to sixteenth-century life and
the hopes with which English men and women first emigrated to North
America.

Professor David Sutton Phelps of East Carolina University showed
me his excavations of Choanoke Indian sites and shared his understanding of pre-contact Carolina Algonquian culture with me. Jane
Blanshard and Joel Kupperman read the entire manuscript and made
many helpful suggestions. Sara Rogers was my invaluable guide
through the thickets of word-processing technology. Though all these
people have aided me, none is responsible for any errors that remain in
the manuscript.

Through quadricentennial celebrations in the 1980's Americans will
become more aware of their country's origins in the 1580's, especially
of the drama of the colonists' lives. One attraction of Roanoke to me is
that the people come alive through the documents they left behind and
we can to some extent feel their feelings and think their thoughts.
Though their assumptions about such matters as the correct way to
organize a society were very different from ours, the elemental emo-
tions surrounding birth and death, love and hate, and the human
response to hardship are more universal and our understanding can
span the centuries. In order to make these men and women speak to
modern readers more clearly, I have modernized their spelling in quota-
tions to eliminate the inevitable feeling of quaintness and even child-
ishness that we unconsciously have when confronting idiosyncratic
sixteenth-century spellings. In all other respects, I have allowed them
to speak for themselves.

1

ENGLAND'S BID FOR GREATNESS

THE story of the Roanoke colony is one of crossed ends and means. Sir Walter Raleigh, who wanted England to be a great nation and had the resources to try to make that dream a reality, believed that plantations in America were a necessary part of greatness. He was the earliest Englishman to make an actual attempt to found colonies in America. In the middle of the 1580s, when Raleigh, a rising young man of thirty, was enjoying the sunshine of the queen's favor, he sent an expedition to the Outer Banks of North Carolina to find a suitable location. When his captains on that venture returned full of enthusiasm for the land, he gathered together a full complement of men and sent them to found the first English settlement in America.

The expedition stayed less than a year, but Raleigh and his closest advisors were still convinced that a plantation could succeed in that location. In 1587, an entirely new conception was tried: a colony composed of families, people who were investing all they had in the venture, was sent to Roanoke. This expedition actually had all the ingredients for success. Later experience proved that only plantations organized in families lasted. Moreover, the new group had the backing of a corporation in England, which was necessary to provide continuous support. Despite everything, however, this venture, like the previous one, failed. And, whereas the first colonists had managed to get back to England, the men, women, and children of the second were abandoned. The lost colonists of Roanoke disappeared into the American continent never to be seen again by Europeans.

Why did Raleigh, convinced as he was of the importance of his venture, allow it to fail? The answer lies in the problem of ends and means. No one knew precisely what a colony was to be for; investors had many different and sometimes conflicting views about its purpose.

Everyone had unrealistic ideas about how much effort and support would be required to found a settlement that could stand on its own. Many were not even convinced that it should have an independent existence; some backers thought of the colony purely as a military outpost that would always be somewhat tentative in nature. When events demonstrated to investors just how unrealistic their thinking was, many pulled back and put their support into projects whose outcome was more certain.

English attention later returned to the founding of American plantations, but it took many decades and more failures before promoters worked out a formula for success based on a clear set of goals. The irony of Roanoke is that the colony would never have been undertaken without the unrealistic aims of its promoters, yet it was the incompatibility of their various hopes that killed it. No sixteenth-century English colony was successful; most did not get beyond the talking stage. Yet these early attempts contained all the models for successful colonization and illustrated all the pitfalls. Some lessons were learned quickly and easily; others had to be experienced several times. But the Roanoke colonies pointed the way for all subsequent English plantations. This was also true of the people involved; in these early voyages we see the archetypes of the men and women who eventually founded British America. Many of the characters in the Roanoke story seem just that, archetypes, people who are larger than life. They are among the most heroic actors in a heroic age, the England of Queen Elizabeth I, when little England faced up to the Spanish giant, and arts and learning flourished. This is the age of Shakespeare and Sir Francis Drake, and of Sir Walter Raleigh, poet, historian, and man of action.

A major goal of all voyages to America was to attack the possessions of Philip II, the king of Spain. The patriotic English gentry believed that the cornerstone of the country's policy was opposition to the Iberians. England was the leader of the Protestant forces in Europe, as Spain was of the Roman Catholic; and the latter's strength, based partly on the immense wealth garnered from its American plantations, was very great. England, by comparison, was weak and backward. Men like Sir Walter Raleigh, who wanted the country to be strong and respected, believed that an English presence in America was an absolute necessity. On the other hand, many of the most important British leaders, including the queen, argued that dividing England's resources would lead to greater weakness. Elizabeth was willing to put her government's money into Protestant causes on the continent of Europe, though cautiously, but not into American ventures.

The government, including Elizabeth, was only too willing to see English people attempt to establish a foothold in America, though, and to give whatever informal backing they could. It became a cardinal point of policy that all enterprises in the Atlantic must be financed and fostered by private enterprise. If a venture looked particularly promising, Elizabeth and her counselors might invest some of their own funds in it but never the government's. Foreign policy always depended to some extent on the profit motive.

England had been involved in American expeditions from the time the new land's existence had been known, but not in a way that would lead to colonization. English ships, along with vessels from all over Europe, went every summer to the rich fishing grounds off the Newfoundland Banks. The annual influx, amounting to as many as five hundred ships, had been occurring since at least the very early 1500s, and French and Basque ships had established fisheries on the St. Lawrence River following explorations there by Cartier and Roberval in the 1530s and 1540s; but in both areas the visits were strictly seasonal. The only sustained European presence in the New World was farther south, in Latin America, where the Spanish and Portuguese had come as conquerors. In the 1580s, some English leaders began to argue strongly that England would never take its rightful place among the nations of Europe until it also had founded an outpost in America. They argued that God had reserved the area north of Florida and south of the St. Lawrence for England and Protestantism.

What was different about the situation in the 1580s that generated interest in colonies? England was adopting a new set of roles in world politics, for which colonies were important. America was attractive to English policy-makers because activity there could foster other goals, not as an end in itself. We are accustomed to thinking of England as it later became, the ruler of the seas; but in the late sixteenth century this glory was still a long way off. England was a weak, somewhat backward nation clinging to the fringe of the European continent; the poet John Donne was later to picture his country as the "suburbs" of Europe. Foreign policy involved maneuvering between the super-powers, Spain and France, and trying to avoid involvement in expensive continental wars. Queen Elizabeth, who was a master of the art of keeping her options open, hated war because it irrevocably attached her to one policy, one set of allies. Furthermore, England lacked the resources for all-out war.

For centuries, France had been England's most threatening enemy, but this situation was changing. France was being torn apart by internal conflict between Catholic and Protestant forces. Meanwhile, Philip II, the Hapsburg ruler of Spain, with the fabulous wealth of the Incas and Aztecs flowing into his coffers, was consolidating his power and centralizing control of his European possessions. Spain annexed Portugal and began to tighten its grip on the Low Countries, which had formerly been more loosely held. The Netherlands revolted against the repression this involved, and Spain sent forces in to crush the rebellion. England was now faced with a hostile Spanish presence directly across the channel and the necessity of making a decision about whether to become involved or not. Suddenly the most threatening power on the continent was not France, as in the past, but the formerly remote Spain.

Much more was at stake than military conflict. The Reformation of the early sixteenth century had irrevocably changed all relationships. Since Henry VIII had broken with the Roman Catholic church, England had been through many shifts of religion; but the accession of his daughter, Elizabeth, and her very long reign had established Protestantism as the religion of the country. With France divided on the question of religion, Spain became the protector of Catholicism in Europe, and England led the Protestant nations. England was forced, slowly and reluctantly, to become activist in foreign policy; the revolt of the Protestant Netherlanders against Spanish repression and religious persecution helped to force the issue. England, after tortuous maneuvering, ultimately came to the open aid of Holland.

We should not underestimate the emotional force of this confrontation between Christians, which has been compared to the Cold War of the twentieth century. Each side believed the other was absolved by its religion of all normal moral and ethical behavior in dealing with the enemy, and capable of the most heinous plots. Philip II's commitment to Catholicism was so rigid that Spain could not even tolerate Protestant English ambassadors in the country. England allowed more latitude: not only were there some Roman Catholics, many of them of aristocratic families, but most degrees of Protestantism, from high church Anglicanism to Puritanism, were normally tolerated. All who did not conform to the established church lived with the threat but rarely the actuality of persecution.

English people of this period believed that Spain's goal was nothing less than to crush England and bring the English' people back under the control of the Catholic church. They also believed that this was to be accomplished through an international conspiracy led by Spain, "the sword of that Antichrist of Rome," using English Catholics as agents inside the country. The most prominent Catholic in England was Mary Stuart, the deposed queen of Scotland, who had been raised in France. Mary was a prisoner in England, but various agents still had access to her, and Spain had begun to cultivate contacts in Scotland, then a separate country that had long resisted English domination and whose people held little love for their neighbors to the south. One Spanish plan called for invasion through Scotland in the expectation that English Catholics and the "silent majority" they assumed were still at heart loyal to the old church would rise up and support their "liberators." Enmity between the two nations came to a head in 1584 when the Spanish ambassador, Mendoza, who had been heavily involved in plotting, was expelled, and England broke diplomatic relations with Spain. Elizabeth gave up the freedom of movement and flexibility in international affairs that she loved and prepared for war. In this she was far behind her subjects and advisors, whose hatred of Spain was intense and profound.[1]

America had a part to play in this struggle. Spain was dependent on the flow of treasure that came annually from the Indies. With these riches, the Spanish government had enlarged its scope and centralized its empire, and had embarked on the expensive wars that Elizabeth avoided. Spain was now fatally overcommitted, so that the treasure fleets were a lifeline without whose sustenance the government would collapse. Attacking those heavily laden ships was an ideal way to strike a blow at that empire. Elizabeth, who guarded her control of policy so closely at home, allowed almost complete freedom of action to those who attacked Spain in the Indies and on the homeward routes.

Both countries made decisions in 1585. Spain, in retaliation for the expulsion of Ambassador Mendoza, seized those English ships unlucky enough to be caught in Spanish ports. England sent Sir Francis Drake

at the head of a fleet to the West Indies to inflict as much damage and
take as much plunder as he could. For England, this was the opening
of a major sea war. From 1585 to the peace of 1604, increasing
numbers of privateers, as many as one hundred a year, were licensed to
prey on the Spanish treasure ships for their own and the country's
enrichment. Spain attempted to meet the challenge by redesigning the
fleet, using fast, maneuverable individual ships called *galizabras* to
carry treasure, instead of large, slow-moving convoys of clumsy transport ships escorted by men-of-war. Anger over the depredations
strengthened Spanish desire to cut off the harassment at its source by
sending the Great Armada against England in 1588. The Armada,
fatally flawed by poor planning and inadequate equipment, failed; and
the treasure fleet's new evasive strategy was only partly fruitful.
Despite all attempts to foil them, many English privateering voyages
were highly successful, and Spain's hold on the West Indies was
significantly weakened by their cumulative effect.

Privateering had originated as a way for merchants to recover the
value of cargoes lost on the high seas. The procedure was originally
very tightly controlled. The government issued letters of reprisal, good
for six months, which authorized the holder to seize Spanish goods
to the amount lost. In order to get a letter of reprisal, the shipowner
had to have witnesses who could describe his losses and their cause
accurately and convincingly. This system kept the government out of
conflicts because the action of the merchants was considered completely private; in practice, the government took a share of each prize
captured, and Queen Elizabeth invested in privateering ventures as a
private person.

Enforcement of the rules was becoming increasingly lax and corrupt,
and eventually merchants and promoters simply bought letters from
the authorities or from legitimate owners, or even went out without
licenses. Official corruption protected them from the consequences of
such practices. In theory, privateering was distinct from simple piracy
because it was limited to a specific enemy and had government authori-
zation. In practice, this line became extremely fuzzy during the late
sixteenth century, and many English mariners preyed on any ships they
thought they could take. During this period, the scope of privateering
also changed. Whereas formerly it had been largely limited to small-
scale action in the English Channel, now major fleets sailed for the
West Indies and the biggest game of all.

Privateering involved strange alliances between long-established and newly prominent groups. Each voyage was put together by a joint-stock company, an early form of corporation, that existed only for the life of the venture. Its main advantage was the ability to amass large amounts of capital for outfitting the ships while minimizing the risk for each investor. Joint-stock companies, a relatively new device, were used to finance everything from colonies to Shakespeare's Globe Theatre.

The earliest privateering ventures in the open sea war against Spain were combinations of traders, who had ships and access to letters of reprisal, and gentlemen. The coming of the gentry to this field of action completely transformed it. For them, privateering meant a chance to extricate themselves from financial difficulties. Many were being squeezed because their incomes, based on rents, could not keep up with the rate of inflation. If they lived at court, they were expected to maintain an extravagant, free-spending life that few could sustain indefinitely. They liked privateering because it had the style of a grand project, of gambling for the highest stakes. One really successful voyage could make their fortunes, though they could also be wiped out. Furthermore, it was not mere money-grubbing. When conflict with Spain became open war, preying on the Spanish treasure fleets came to be seen as a patriotic gesture, striking at England's enemy and bringing glory to daring men and to the country. They also saw it as defense of the true faith, and many of their ships had religious names such as *Grace of God, Blessing of God, Gift of God, Holy Ghost, John Evangelist,* and *Seraphim.* The Spanish treasure ships had such names as *Buen Jesús* and *Madre de Dios.*

Sir Walter Raleigh, the promoter of the Roanoke colonies, shared these goals. He was one of the few successful gentlemen in this early phase of the privateering war. He saw that the greatest chances of gain lay in alliance with the great merchants, and he was one of the first to move in that direction. He was unusual among gentleman-adventurers in being able to operate on the scale of the most powerful merchants. The gentry-dominated ventures rarely paid off, because neither the gentlemen nor the small traders with whom they were typically allied had the knowledge necessary for success, especially as the gentlemen, whether they were experienced or not, demanded the swashbuckling role of leaders of the expeditions.

The merchants initially stayed in the background; they lent money to privateering companies but did not invest. When merchants began to invest openly, they took control of the ventures and organized them in businesslike fashion. They furnished the ships and hired the men to control the fleets. Because most of the merchants involved in privateering had originally been in the Iberian trades, and many of them had lost heavily when Spain seized English ships, their desire for vengeance was strong. They had tremendous advantages over the gentlemen in buying supplies and disposing of plunder, and they had large fleets at their command. Privateering became very profitable in their hands and activities became centralized.

John Watts was an example of the success possible in this field. He came to London as a teenager, probably as an apprentice, and married the daughter of a leading London merchant, an enormously advantageous match. Watts went into business with his father-in-law and brother-in-law and gained experience as a factor, or agent, for the company in Spain in the 1570s and early 1580s. He lost heavily in the Spanish confiscation of English ships in 1585 and sued for letters of reprisal. Watts went wholeheartedly into privateering, sending out numerous ships every year; but he continued to engage in ordinary trading. He became tremendously rich and was knighted when King James I came to the throne in 1603; in 1606–1607 he was Lord Mayor of London and entertained the king at his home. He had a distinguished career for someone who was described to the Spanish king as "the greatest pirate that has ever been in this kingdom." Patriotic and religious motives were important for merchants like Watts; he not only sent a ship, the *Margaret and John,* to join the fleet that confronted the Armada, but he also sailed on it as a volunteer and participated in the worst of the fighting. Watts also exemplified the connection between colonization and privateering: he was involved in the attempt to locate and rescue the lost colonists of Roanoke and was very active in promoting the first successful colony, Jamestown.

Most merchants combined privateering and legitimate trade. Privateers were usually large trading vessels called merchantmen with a few guns added and extremely large crews. Merchantmen usually traveled in consort with a smaller ship, a pinnace, that could be powered by sails or oars and was useful for approaching and boarding a prize ship because of its flexibility and ease of handling. The ships might go on a trading voyage one year and be sent privateering the next; or they might even combine both functions in a single trip, marauding after the cargo was sold. The large crew was necessary for subduing and boarding prizes. And, as ships were captured, mariners from the privateers were detailed to man the newly acquired vessels and sail them home to England. Victualing such crowded ships was very expensive.

The huge crews were extremely difficult to control. They received no wages and signed on for one-third of the take, which was divided among them by a formula based on rank and service. In addition, they had rights of "pillage," which meant that they could take anything that was on the deck of a captured vessel; in practice, they felt entitled to anything that was loose in the ship. Sometimes, they "broke bulk"–that is, they broke into the prize cargo and plundered it, cheating the customs and their investors. Conditions were extremely bad on these ships, and they became worse as the voyage progressed and the food and beer went bad or simply ran out. The overcrowded ships were filthy; dysentery, which they called "bloody flux," and scurvy, produced by a diet of salt meat and biscuit that was virtually devoid of fresh food, were rampant. And mariners of course ran the risk of returning empty-handed from a long and arduous voyage if no prizes were taken.

Everyone involved in privateering ran great risks. It mushroomed because it also promised and occasionally brought great rewards, and because it was patriotically aimed at the great enemy, Spain. The ships and experience gained in the sea war at the end of the sixteenth century were crucial for England. These ships belonging to private venturers carried on the naval side of the war against Spain; there was virtually no separate government force. The gentlemen and merchants who sent out ships of prey were the representatives of the crown, and those in high office who pushed the anti-Spanish foreign policy also outfitted and sent out the privateers. They could only revel in the assurance that private gain and public good were both served by the same action.[2]

Sir Walter Raleigh, a second son born in 1554, came from an old and distinguished but relatively poor family of Devon in the West of England. As was common in that era when life was so uncertain, both his parents had been married before, and Raleigh was connected to many of the most important families in the region. His father had been married to a Drake. His mother, who was his father's third wife, came from a family, the Champernownes, that had connections with the sea; her brother was vice-admiral for Devon. John, Humphrey, and Adrian

Gilbert, her sons by her previous husband, Otho Gilbert, were all interested in seafaring; young Raleigh was inspired by the actions and plans of his half-brothers, whose interests he came to share. Raleigh had a short childhood and no adolescence. He was registered at Oriel College, Oxford, in 1568 when he was fourteen and stayed on the rolls until 1572; but for much of that time he was actually in France fighting on the side of the Protestant Huguenots with a large company of West Country gentlemen, many of them his relatives. This was a vicious war, with savage reprisals conducted by both sides, a harsh introduction to adult roles for the teenaged Raleigh.

He returned to London and registered at England's law school, the Inns of Court. Many English gentlemen spent a year or two there, especially if they expected to own landed estates in the future, because lawsuits were ubiquitous, and the head of a family had to know how to maneuver his way through the courts. One did not take formal classes at the Inns of Court; rather the student lived in the lawyers' environment and absorbed some idea of legal principles and procedures. How much the student learned depended on his diligence. Raleigh may have learned more about geography and the prospects for colonization than he did about law, because the Middle Temple, his Inn, was home to one of the earliest and most important proponents of the idea that England should seek greatness through overseas empire, Richard Hakluyt the elder. Raleigh later claimed he had never read a word of law; most of his time was spent in literary circles, where he was prized for his brilliance of wit. He began publishing poetry during this time, balancing his military skills by cultivating the other side of his character.

Many Elizabethan gentlemen combined action in war and colonization with literary interests. Raleigh's half-brother, Sir Humphrey Gilbert, published a call to empire in 1576, "proving" that there must be a passage through the American continent to Asia. In 1578, he received a patent to colonize the coast of North America and set out with a fleet whose main, but hidden, purpose was to harass Spanish shipping. Raleigh was on this expedition in command of the *Falcon,* with a Portuguese navigator named Simon Fernandes as his pilot. Since Raleigh was young and completely inexperienced at sea, his appointment aptly illustrates the principle universally accepted in Elizabethan times that social status was more important than skill in command.

The fleet was forced by storms to turn back shortly after leaving England, but Raleigh refused to go home before he had tasted action; his eventual encounter with a Spanish ship was a near-disaster, and much of his crew was killed. In order to make his flamboyant gesture, Raleigh sacrificed many sailors.

Such carelessness with the lives of the men and women of humble station who served under them was common among the heroic gentry of the Elizabethan era. Often their celebrated exploits were bought at enormous cost in human life, a fact usually omitted from the myths that grew up around these figures. On the other hand, the men who sailed on Raleigh's ships throughout his life seem to have been the only people outside his immediate family who truly loved him. In 1583 Gilbert tried again, heading an ill-fated expedition that attempted to found a colony in Newfoundland or New England. This venture ended with Gilbert's death at sea, which proved the truth of Queen Elizabeth's observation that he was a man "of no good hap at sea." By the time of Gilbert's second voyage, Raleigh had become the new favorite of the queen, and she had forbidden him to sail on such a dangerous mission.

After the continental wars and command at sea, one set of experiences remained to complete Raleigh's education in the manner of the aspiring gentleman, service in Ireland, the site of England's first true colonies. In 1580, he went to Munster as a captain of infantry, to put down the rebellion of the Desmonds. Here many of his several sides showed themselves clearly. He participated in brutal reprisals, for example supervising the executions of the entire population of Smerwick, six hundred people, in a single day when the garrison succumbed to an English siege. Irish sources maintain that the fortress had been guaranteed their lives would be spared if they surrendered. Raleigh agreed with his superiors that the way to settle the Irish problem was unremitting use of force. Typically he also engaged in daring and dangerous exploits. His ambition and arrogance were clearly evident in his letters home to the government harshly criticizing his superiors in Ireland and outlining his ideas of the proper conduct of the campaign.

Raleigh was back in England in 1581, and here his meteoric rise began. Up to this time, he had traveled the common path of a young English gentleman with aspirations. Now, he marked himself out as different. Somehow, he caught the queen's attention; his biographers are not willing to rule out the story, written many years after his death, of his spreading his best plush cloak over a puddle before the queen. If the story is true, the sacrifice of his cloak was repaid many hundreds of times over. Queen Elizabeth was no more willing to spend money on those she favored at home than she was on foreign adventures, but she had ways of rewarding them. Raleigh received, over the course of the next decade, vast estates in Ireland and very large holdings all over England. Moreover, she bestowed a sure source of income on him by giving him the patent on wines and the license for the exporting of woolen cloth, which gave him monopoly control of these industries. Raleigh's agents made the patents pay. He raked off £1,200 a year from the vintners, and the woolen cloth export monopoly paid £3,500 in a good year. These monopolies were very bitterly resented, especially by merchants, and Raleigh's agents were particularly zealous in collecting everything due him.

He was also given various government offices, particularly in his own West Country. The office of which he was proudest was his captaincy of the guard, because it entailed constant attendance on the queen. Raleigh became a very wealthy man; otherwise he would never have been able to dream of colonization. But his American adventures also drained off much of his fortune and ultimately brought him to disaster.

During the 1580s, when his power was greatest, Raleigh was naturally the center of an admiring circle, but he was never liked. He was considered too proud, ruthless, and arrogant. Raleigh himself apparently cared for no one's opinion except Elizabeth's. He dressed flamboyantly in rich silks and with large pearl earrings, cultivating his naturally exotic looks. He was, as John Aubrey wrote of him after his death, "damnable proud." The queen apparently loved his flamboyance, but especially his brilliance of mind. He was a master of the punning word games the Elizabethans relished and was able to play the role of respectful but enamored suitor that Elizabeth demanded of her favorites.

Raleigh received one further monopoly, the most important of all for our purposes. In 1584, the year he was knighted, Elizabeth bestowed on him the patent for colonization in America that had lapsed with Sir Humphrey Gilbert's death. His exclusive license meant that no Englishman could venture to North America south of Newfoundland unless he had Raleigh's permission, which he would never give without an agreement to split the proceeds of the expedition. Raleigh was prepared to justify his monopoly by vigorous action. He threw himself wholeheartedly into promoting his overseas adventures and worked to involve as many of England's intellectual and financial leaders as he could. He sent out a reconnoitering voyage soon after his patent was granted, not to the north that Gilbert had favored, but to the region from which the Spanish treasure fleet could be attacked, the Outer Banks of North Carolina, where he decided to plant his settlement. The Roanoke colonies were the projects of his highest-riding years.[3]

The desire to establish colonies in America was inseparable in these early years from involvement in privateering. When Raleigh decided to found the colony at Roanoke, his major reason was that it could serve as a base for privateering. Expeditions were confined to a very few months of the year by the long winter storm season. Ships left England in the early spring, as soon as they thought they were safe from Atlantic storms. Spring and early summer were the prime period for attacking Spanish shipping. When the hurricane season began in late July, ship captains had to make a close decision between the danger and the chance for gain if they took the risk of staying longer. Having a nearby base would mean that ships could spend a year or more in the Caribbean, calling in at Roanoke for supplies and refitting as needed and attacking enemy vessels whenever the opportunity was offered.

The link with privateering was extremely fateful for Roanoke and the English people who were sent there. It determined the choice of site—near enough to the West Indies to be useful as a base, and yet so secluded that it would be difficult for pursuing Spaniards to find. Unfortunately, as we shall see, it was a poor place in which to develop a plantation. That the colony was linked with privateering also influenced the choice of settlers. Raleigh's first colonists were largely veterans of the Irish or European wars. Their experience meant they would be able to defend the settlement, especially against the Spanish, but would be extremely poor at building a society and maintaining the good relationships with the Indians that were crucial to success. Finally, it disastrously affected the behavior of those who were sent to their aid. In fact, the connection of the settlement and privateering sealed the doom both of the colony and the final group of colonists, those who were abandoned there in 1587. The irony of this failure is that the Roanoke ventures would never have been possible without that connection. Privateering both made the colony attractive and paid for its establishment. Without it, there would not have been an English plantation in America in the sixteenth century.

2

THE FIRST COLONY:
A MILITARY OUTPOST

ROANOKE was intended to be parasitic; its reason for existence was the Spanish treasure fleet, which was in its turn parasitic on the Indian peoples of Central and South America. England's interest was newly directed to the south; all attention had previously been focused on Newfoundland. The summer experience of the fishing fleet had given no hint that winter temperatures of that land, which was, after all, south of London, would seem very cold to Englishmen accustomed to their own maritime climate. Gilbert's failed attempt in 1583 aimed to found a colony in the area thought most comfortable for the English, and to control the activities of the fishermen who came there from all over Europe. These seemed to be realistic goals for an English venture in the 1580s, but Raleigh did not follow them.

When he decided to direct his colonizing activities to the south, Raleigh was purposely venturing into the middle of Spain's own interests. The Spanish had long believed that the North American coastline, at least from Chesapeake Bay south, was part of their natural sphere of influence. They had made a few halfhearted attempts to found colonies in Florida, as they called the entire region, in the first half of the sixteenth century. It was not until the 1560s, when French Protestants, seeking a religious refuge as English Puritans later would, made settlements at Fort Caroline in modern Florida and Charlesfort on Port Royal Sound in South Carolina, that Spain became seriously interested. The French colonies were "extinguished" and St. Augustine was founded. Spanish authorities erected a series of forts on the coast, including one on Parris Island off the coast of modern South Carolina.

Their explorations had convinced the Spanish that Chesapeake Bay was a natural location for a major colony. Spanish Jesuits had sent a mission there in 1570–1571, which the Indians had promptly destroyed, thus gaining a reputation for being fierce and warlike. Still, Chesapeake Bay, with its sheltered deepwater ports, was considered by those who had explored it to be the most promising site for a settlement. Raleigh, who had some knowledge of the desirability of the great bay, did not send his initial expedition there because it was far away from the West Indies and the homeward course of the treasure fleet. Moreover, once the colony began operating as a privateering base, he knew Spanish warships would be looking for it and with their knowledge of Chesapeake Bay would be able to find a settlement there easily. The awesome reputation of the Indians may also have contributed to the decision to put the first English colony farther south.

Raleigh's first expedition under his new patent left as soon as he could arrange it. Two ships, under the command of Philip Amadas and Arthur Barlowe, left the west of England on April 27th, 1584. They took the normal southern route, picking up the trade winds off the Canaries and sailing west to the Caribbean, from which they moved up the coast. They sighted mainland North America on July 4th and landed on July 13th off North Carolina on the line of coastal islands, actually little more than sandbars, known as the Outer Banks. Their landfall was at an inlet into the shallow sounds beyond the Banks later called Hatarask, but which they named Port Ferdinando after their Portuguese pilot, Simon Fernandes, whom they credited with discovering it. This was the same Fernandes who had been Raleigh's pilot in 1578.

Amadas and Barlowe were not sent to establish a colony; their mission was to reconnoiter and find a suitable area for settlement, and they believed they had accomplished that when they discovered Roanoke Island sheltered between the mainland and the Outer Banks. They returned full of enthusiasm for the place and its possibilities, as can be seen in Barlowe's account of the mission's discoveries. Though they had done little actual exploring or testing, he wrote in the most glowing terms of the possibilities of the new land: "The soil is the most plentiful, sweet, fruitful, and wholesome of all the world." They brought back two very impressive Indians, said to be volunteers, Manteo and Wanchese, who were invaluable to Raleigh's propaganda efforts for his first full colony.

The difficulty of learning anything reliable about the territory by interrogating Indians whose language they did not know was well illustrated by the array of names given to the new land. Amadas and Barlowe proclaimed that the Indian name of the territory was *Wingandacoia*, sometimes Europeanized to *Wingan de Coy*. Raleigh later explained that this name, which was widely publicized, was the result of a misunderstanding. What the Indians had really said was, "you wear good clothes, or gay clothes." Raleigh's correction apparently introduced another mistake; modern linguists believe the Indians were giving the name of some sweet-smelling evergreens at which they thought the explorers were pointing. Manteo and Wanchese apparently learned English readily and taught some Algonquian to Thomas Hariot, who accompanied the 1585 expedition, so understanding was much greater in later expeditions. It was ultimately decided that the Indian name for the area was *Ossomocomuck*.

The real difficulty with Barlowe's account is his desire to make Roanoke attractive, to make it interesting to colonists and backers. He not only praised the supposed great fruitfulness of the island, but recklessly compared it to the Garden of Eden: "The earth bringeth forth all things in abundance, as in the first creation, without toil or labor." Barlowe wanted to convince people in England that this part of America was a good site for an English colony, but he, like all people interested in promotion, ran the risk of elevating expectations too high and causing people to come unprepared for the actual hardships and limitations in settling this land. People who came to America expecting life to be easy were difficult to control once they realized the true situation. Every colony had to cope with the fact that disaffected people, on their return to England, would tell their tales of hardship and deprivation to everyone who would listen and make the country seem worse than it was. Colonial promoters learned slowly and painfully that it was better to describe the country as truthfully as possible, detailing the disadvantages as well as the advantages, in order to forestall as much as possible the rebound effect of disillusioned settlers complaining in pubs throughout England. The story of Roanoke is a tale of unreasonable and conflicting goals and expectations that frustrated each other and made all planning go awry, and reports such as Barlowe's added to the problem. The ultimate result was the tragedy of the Lost Colony.

All this was in the future, however. When Amadas and Barlowe returned from their reconnaissance mission of 1584, all signs looked promising for a permanent settlement off North Carolina. Backers in England were assured that the land was good. More importantly, the Outer Banks seemed to be an ideal spot for the kind of activities they had in mind—close enough to the trade routes to give easy access and yet hidden away from the Spanish in Florida. Everything written about the area in these early years was deliberately vague in order to preserve the mystery of its exact location. Even Sir Francis Drake, who came to aid the colony, was not completely sure how to find it.

Backers were being signed up for the next expedition and plans were well underway even before Amadas and Barlowe returned. Raleigh was able to attract many influential men to the project, especially once the reconnoitering fleet with Manteo and Wanchese aboard was back in England. Raleigh's initiative was viewed with approval by government officials such as Sir Francis Walsingham, leader of those among the queen's advisors who wanted her to follow a frank anti-Spanish policy, even to the extent of openly espousing the cause of beleaguered Protestants in the Netherlands and France. Walsingham was the queen's principal secretary and the master of a vast and efficient spy system within England and throughout Europe. As a principal advisor, he was freed from the playful courtier's role played by men like Raleigh, and his advice was taken seriously. Walsingham increasingly sponsored those who promoted colonization and the naval strength and expertise that went with it, and his influence was crucial to the success of many ventures. His own sons-in-law, Sir Philip Sidney and Christopher Carleill, were both heavily involved in overseas ventures.

Queen Elizabeth herself gave the project many marks of favor. She knighted Raleigh, the chief mover, and even allowed the territory to be called Virginia in her honor, thus eliminating embarrassment over the Wingandacoia fiasco. She also invested in the expedition, and her ship, the *Tiger,* was its admiral or flagship. Elizabeth gave Raleigh the right to seize men and prize ships, a power Parliament had refused to grant him. Finally, she released Ralph Lane, who was to be governor of the new colony, from his service in Ireland, while continuing to pay his salary.

Five major ships and two pinnaces left Plymouth on April 9th, 1585, sailing by way of the Canaries to the West Indies and thence to North

Carolina. Because Elizabeth again refused to allow Raleigh to go to sea, his cousin, Sir Richard Grenville, sailed instead. He was named general of the expedition and admiral of the fleet, despite the fact that he had no naval experience. Grenville's status was somewhat different from that of the other naval heroes of the time. He had had the typical upbringing: education at the Inns of Court, at the Middle Temple, which equipped him to conduct the business normal for the head of a gentry family; and service in foreign wars, in his case Hungary, and in Ireland. Grenville was different in that he began his career as a wealthy and powerful man. He was heir to the very large estates of a family that could trace its importance back at least to the Norman Conquest, and under his care the family's holdings grew even larger. By contrast, the Raleighs were a small and declining family; Walter, as a second son, had to make his own way.

Once he returned from his early training, Grenville had settled down in his family's seat in the West of England and dutifully and competently performed the functions of the local gentry. He worked hard as a member of Parliament, a local justice of the peace, and as sheriff of Cornwall, a particularly important position. One aspect of his job that he took very seriously was the rooting out of hidden nests of Catholics. He was knighted after his term as sheriff, and the government increasingly found itself turning to him for advice or action when affairs in the West of England required attention. Grenville was in his mid-forties when he sailed for America. He still had the reputation, acquired in his youth, of being hot-tempered and forceful in his actions; he had killed another gentleman in a London street brawl before he was twenty-one.

Grenville's appointment exemplifies a fundamental fact of life in Elizabethan times, one that would plague all colonial ventures. Though there must have been many seasoned veterans on board those ships, the man with the highest social standing, regardless of experience or competence, would be at the top. And he would actually command. Again and again in the colonies we see examples of more humble men accepting orders to do things that they knew would bring disaster but were forced to do by the conventions of their times. Grenville was a competent leader in England, but he had no experience of sea voyages, and especially not of the problems of trans-Atlantic ventures.

Second in military command was the high marshall, Thomas Cavendish, a young man of about twenty five, who later repeated Drake's feat of circumnavigating the globe. Below him was Ralph Lane, an equerry of the queen, who stayed on as the first Governor of Roanoke. On the naval side, the vice-admiral was twenty-one year old Philip Amadas, who remained as admiral of the colony, followed by the ubiquitous Simon Fernandes. Fernandes, the pilot, was a Protestant Portuguese from the Azores. Many on the expedition disliked the fact that such a crucial position as chief pilot and master of the flagship, the *Tiger,* was held by a foreigner, particularly as he had previously served the Spanish in these same waters. Nevertheless, his experience and skill were too valuable to dispense with, and he was a protege of Lane and Walsingham.[1] Scattered throughout the ships were various gentlemen, friends, neighbors, and kinsmen of Grenville and Raleigh. Some of these also remained in the colony. The seven ships carried six hundred men, about half of whom were sailors. The fact that the crews were so large was a sure indicator of an intention to combine privateering with their other mission; only one hundred and seven men were eventually left in the colony.

A great storm scattered the fleet at sea and one of the pinnaces was lost, so the *Tiger* stopped at Puerto Rico to build a new one. The expedition clearly needed such a small, maneuverable ship for a variety of reasons. Although the pinnace or longboat was important for exploring the shallow coastal waters around Roanoke, it was mostly needed for privateering.

The ship's crew set out to perform an enormous task in the midst of hostile territory, and the speed and efficiency with which it was done gives invaluable insight into their ability to cope with unforeseen situations. They rapidly built a strong earthwork fort, 1150 feet by 950 feet, for their short stay, and set up a forge to make nails. They arrived on the island on May 11th or 12th and began work on May 13th on the pinnace, for which trees were cut as much as three miles away and hauled to the fort on a truck, the wheels or rollers used to carry their heavy ordnance on shipboard. Despite the size and complexity of the operation, the pinnace was finished on May 23rd, and left the island on May 24th with the *Tiger* and Cavendish's ship, which had arrived on the 19th. Before leaving, the men destroyed their fort. The three ships spent the next several weeks privateering and doing some trading in the West Indies. They also picked up some livestock and plants for the prospective colonists.

During the sojourn in the West Indies, a bitter quarrel erupted between Grenville and Lane, and both wrote to their allies in England about it. Lane accused Grenville of endangering his life, because the admiral had sent him and a small party of men to take some Spanish salt on Puerto Rico. Salt was an essential commodity for preservation of food and was therefore valuable. It was produced by evaporation of sea water in ponds where the climate was suitable. Lane found some salt mounds, surrounded them with earthworks, and set his men to carrying off as much as they could. They were approached by armed Spaniards, though not challenged, and in retrospect Lane felt Grenville had been unreasonable in commanding him and his men to take such risks.

Moreover, he claimed that Grenville threatened to execute him for mutiny because he had publicly given advice in the council. The council consisted of the military and naval hierarchy together with the various ship's captains and gentlemen on the voyage. The best naval practice involved close cooperation between council and commander; Drake, for example, consulted his council on all important decisions during his simultaneous West Indian expedition. The inexperienced Grenville apparently preferred to govern alone, even taking on powers not really his. Not only was Lane alienated, but Thomas Cavendish, the high marshall, who was supposed to have supreme judicial power and to share command, was also among Grenville's enemies in the company. Lane said Grenville was tyrannical and referred to his "intolerable pride."

It is possible that the underlying cause of the quarrel and the subject of Lane's advice may have been the fleet's long sojourn in the West Indies. Lane complained that they landed in Roanoke much too late to do all that was necessary in preparation for the colony's first winter. Lane had powerful friends in England, and Fernandes, who shared his feeling about Grenville, was a member of Sir Francis Walsingham's household. Lane poured out his side of the story in letters to Walsingham, who removed his influence from the Virginia project from that time forward, though he continued his interest in exploration and colonization.[2]

The diminished fleet arrived off the Outer Banks at Wococon, a now-vanished inlet through Portsmouth Island south of Roanoke, on

June 26th, where they found that others of their company had arrived before them. At Wococon they began to understand for the first time the inadequacy of their chosen site. Roanoke Island is surrounded by shallow sounds totally unsuitable as anchorages for the larger English vessels; Roanoke Sound is to the east, Croatan to the west, Albemarle to the north. These three drain into Pamlico' Sound to the south. Depths today range upwards from one foot; the average depth in Roanoke Sound is five feet, and that of Croatan is nine feet. In the 1580s, the Outer Banks were one mile east of their present location, so Roanoke Sound was wider and deeper, while Croatan Sound was shallow and marshy. One report said it was possible to walk across Croatan Sound to the mainland on the small islands and hummocks. Amadas and Barlowe had traveled along the east side of Roanoke and around its northern tip, and that became the normal route.

The colonists discovered the three major inlets then in existence in addition to Wococon, which was seventy to eighty miles south of the island. Immediately opposite the southern end of Roanoke were Port Ferdinando, later renamed Hatarask, and Port Lane, separated by a small island a league long. These have been replaced by the modern Oregon inlet. Twenty-five miles to the north, near modern Duck, was Trinity Harbor, the third entrance. Hatarask became the most important anchorage, and the colonists developed a slipway there to get supplies across. It was eight to twelve feet deep at high tide and could shelter ships of seventy tons and allow twenty-ton vessels over the bar into the sound; but navigation through the channel was difficult and dangerous. The mariners quickly discovered that the larger English ships, such as the *Tiger* at one hundred and sixty tons, were forced to anchor several miles off shore completely exposed to the Atlantic and its storms.[3]

At their first anchorage the *Tiger* was forced against the banks at Wococon repeatedly, so that the sailors feared losing the ship entirely. As it was, most of the food supplies for the new colony were lost. A member of the *Tiger's* crew kept a journal, and this anonymous partisan of Grenville's accused Fernandes of recklessness and incompetence. The accident was a major blow to all the plans of settlers and promoters and a grim warning about the site's inadequacy for their purposes.

The great question now was what should be done. There is some evidence that Grenville and his fleet had been expected to stay over the winter and inaugurate Roanoke's use as a privateering base immediately. The destruction of the *Tiger's* stores changed all that. Provisions were now too skimpy for a large force, and it was clear that the present location would not do as a harbor for a major privateering venture. Lane's job would be to use Roanoke as a base from which to search for a suitable harbor and site. When the fleet returned the next year, the plan could be put into operation from a better landing.

Once it was decided that Grenville and the fleet would return to England, leaving just over a hundred men under Ralph Lane to live off the land, the most immediate task was to choose a site for the fort and get started on it, so accommodations would be ready for winter. Lane, who had been chosen for command partly because he was a fortifications expert, began the construction, while Grenville took several boats and the new pinnace and began exploring the coast and rivers of the mainland.

By July 27th, the *Tiger* was once again seaworthy, so the fleet sailed up to Port Ferdinando, where it stayed while the colony's site on the northern end of Roanoke Island was selected and the fort begun. Early in August, Amadas was sent to explore Albemarle Sound, where he stayed about a month, and one of the smallest and fastest ships was sent home to tell Raleigh about the fleet's safe arrival, and to warn him that Grenville was returning to England and that the colony would need new stores quickly to replace those lost when the *Tiger* ran aground.

We have some idea of the settlement's appearance. Plans made in England called for the colonists to build a large fort encompassing all the houses around a market square. The five-sided fort was to be surrounded by a palisade, a solid wall of sawn or split upright boards affixed to two or three horizontal rails nailed to posts set in the ground about nine feet apart. Planners thought the colonists could build such a sound defensive structure within a month.

In fact, the colonists did not follow these instructions. We know they built a fort, which may have had one structure within it, but that the houses were outside the post, though nearby. There were two examples of colonial fortifications that Lane, with his Irish experience, might have followed. One called for the entire town to be encompassed within a palisade, the type suggested by Roanoke's advisors and later used at Jamestown, the first successful English colony in America.

The other model was followed by Lane and his colonists: the "bawne" village, in which a principal building was enclosed in a fort into whose walls the colonists' cattle were driven at night and which would shelter all inhabitants in case of attack. The enemy in the colonists' minds was, of course, Spain, and the fort's guns would have pointed out to sea. By the beginning of September, Lane was dating his letters from the "New fort in Virginia," so the main settlement was completed within a month of their arrival.

Houses, hastily built to shelter the men through the coming winter, were constructed according to traditional methods, which involved the creation of a skeleton of large posts sunk into the ground and joined by horizontal and slanting timbers, with trenched wooden sills. The spaces between the timbers would have been filled in with prefabricated wattle and daub panels made by weaving split saplings around and through upright sticks and covering the entire panel with clay. These half-timbered houses were easily set up and as easily dismantled for carriage to another location. The final colony apparently did take them down and carry them away for use elsewhere. The dirt-floored houses had upper stories or lofts for sleeping and thatched roofs which, especially with wattle and daub chimneys, were quite flammable and dangerous.

The colonists set up a brick-making works almost immediately, but, as six months to a year were required to make bricks of reasonable quality, they would not have been used in the original construction. Some very poor bricks of the local clay have been discovered, suggesting that they may have tried to rush the process, but the clay would not have supported really satisfactory brick-making even with the best procedures. The documents seem to indicate that men of highest status had their own separate cottages, but references to "Mr. Hariot's house," for example, may only mean that he was the head of that household. The documents also speak of a jail and various storehouses. There is no evidence of wells. Colonists may have been dependent on rainwater for their supply of fresh water, possibly from barrels sunk in the sand dunes, or they may have used a nearby creek. The men would have lived in relative comfort in these familiar houses, patterned as they were on English rural cottages. There are several reports of a clothing shortage during the winter, but the reason for that is unclear, unless reserves had been traded to the Indians.[4]

Modern archeological excavations have discovered a diamond-shaped earthwork fort with elongated points on the extreme northern end of Roanoke Island, which dates from the time of the Lane colony. It was built by digging a trench in the shape intended for the fort, using the excavated dirt to build a parapet. The inner floor of the compound was then lowered by about 6 inches, making the wall 6 feet high on the inside. A firing step about 1½ feet high would have been built along the interior wall. This fort, about 50 square feet on the inside, has been reconstructed by the National Park Service and forms the center-piece of the Fort Raleigh National Historic Site. Recent work has uncovered remains of postholes possibly left from the houses or pal-isade of the colonists' village very near to the reconstructed fort. We do not know if Lane's colonists built a defensive wall around their houses, but the next group of colonists occupied the same dwellings and did erect a palisade. The postholes could be from either settle-ment.

The picture gleaned from archaeology confirms that of the documen-tary record: a fortification on the north end of Roanoke Island with an adjoining village of small cottages. Though the boat landing site was two to three miles to the south, on Shallowbag Bay, the letters and memoirs from the colony firmly indicate a settlement on the northern tip. Controversy rages over whether the fort excavated by the Park Ser-vice can actually be Lane's "New fort in Virginia," because it is small and of the type that was so quickly and easily built in the West Indies, and because few artifacts clearly of European manufacture have been discovered in or near it.

It is clear that the present fort is of the period and was probably con-structed by Lane's colonists; but, so the argument goes, it may have been either a temporary structure or an outpost to be manned in case of attack from the north. Some of the controversialists assert that the set-tlement was not at this site at all and that erosion may have taken the land the colonists built on, either to the north or farther south, closer to Shallowbag Bay. It is true that the island is now about four miles less in length than it was then, at least a quarter of a mile of land at the north end having been lost to erosion, and the configuration of Roanoke Island is so changed since the 1580s that the colonists' own descriptions are not clear enough to fix locations with certainty. On the other hand all the documentary evidence strongly points to the north end of the island as the village location. One likely possibility is that the reconstructed fort is actually part of a much larger fort, probably one corner. Defensive structures commonly had such elaborate elongated points or flankers forming at least some of the corners to allow marksmen to shoot along the outside walls. Even the earthworks quickly thrown up in the West Indies by Lane's men had such bastions.[5]

When the ships sailed for home at the end of August, Grenville could report that a very tenuous foothold had been established in America. A settlement was in existence capable of sheltering colonists through the winter and protected more by its seclusion than its fortifications from a Spanish attack. But the loss of supplies in the accident to the *Tiger* meant that the men would be living off the land, which really meant living off Indian largesse. No one knew whether there would be sufficient food supplies for the winter. The backers, though, did not regard the colony as important in itself. The connection with privateering overshadowed all other considerations when Roanoke was viewed from England, and people at home felt they had reason to be pleased with the news even though the harbors at Roanoke were unsuitable for sheltering privateering fleets. By the time the ships returned in the spring, Lane and his men would have found a better location.

The interests of the colony were always seen as secondary, to be sacrificed readily when other concerns, particularly those associated with the sea war, were perceived as pressing. Raleigh had decided to send a second fleet in June to carry further supplies to Roanoke. Those ships, whose supplies were now essential, would have arrived as the colony was being set up and Grenville was departing. Just as the squadron was ready to sail, however, the queen had commanded Raleigh to divert it to Newfoundland to warn the English there that Spain had seized all English ships in Spanish harbors and that a sea war was on. On no account were the fishermen to attempt to sell their catch in the Iberian peninsula, and they must be alert to the danger of sudden Spanish attacks on them. Had the fleet been allowed to sail to Virginia as planned, making up the lost stores, the history of Roanoke would have been very different.

For the colonists, the position must have looked somewhat bleak. From the point of view of the backers, though, the connection of

privateering and colonization received powerful reinforcement from
Raleigh's venture, and many must have decided without much thought
that colonization certainly paid off. Grenville arrived back in England
with some evidence of the area's fertility in the form of plant specimens, and nothing but scorn for the harbors of the Outer Banks. But,
though enthusiasm for the land was muted, expectations for the future
were elevated: Grenville had captured a "very richly laden" prize, the
Santa María de San Vicente. There was tremendous excitement
throughout England at Grenville's success; one gentleman wrote that
all the talk now was of killing Spaniards.

Grenville's exploit seemed more heroic in that the *Tiger* was a ship
of 160 tons, compared to the *Santa María's* 300 tons, and he had no
pinnace with which to board it. He approached his prize in a little
boat put together out of boards taken from chests, which fell apart
"and sunk at the ship's side, as soon as ever he and his men were out of
it." There was controversy over the cargo in England; many reports
said the ship contained a large cargo of gold, silver, and pearls in addition to the ginger, sugar, and hides that Grenville admitted to. But,
whether or not Grenville cheated his fellow investors, the public cargo
was so rich that all the backers saw a handsome return on their investments. The conclusion seemed very clear: privateering, not cultivation
of the mundane products of North America, made colonies pay. Nothing that concerned a colony would ever be allowed to stand in the way
of privateering. The problems and final abandonment of Roanoke stem
from this simple fact of life. On the other hand, the fact that the capture of the *Santa María de San Vicente* "made" the voyage meant there
would be further money for colonies and more interest in promoting
them. Those who saw the limitations of privateering as an avenue to
national power hoped to keep the connection alive only until colonies
could be justified and sustained in their own right. It was quite clear
that without the great gains to be won from privateering, there would
be no money or thought for American colonies.

3

Expectations

Not everyone interested in colonization was so limited in vision or
so greedy for immediate gain as were members of the privateering-
colonization nexus. Some influential people envisioned prospects closer
to the colonies' actual future, though their notions were often very
wide of the mark. They looked forward to plantations that would be
self-sustaining and would produce a surplus to enrich England. No one
knew how long it would take to realize this goal, nor how many false
starts and how much suffering there would be; had they known,
English people would never have embarked on the project. That was
all in the future. In the mid-1580s, promoters believed that success was
just around the corner.

The leading voices in the campaign to articulate realistic goals for
American colonies were two cousins, both named Richard Hakluyt,
who worked in close cooperation with Raleigh. Richard Hakluyt the
elder was a child when his father died, and he was left with a stepmother who quickly married again. Though his father's will designated
him as heir, he was forced to sue his stepmother and stepfather for his
inheritance, when they conspired to cheat him of it. Because life was
so precarious in the sixteenth century, many children lost one or both
parents before their majority and grew up with at least one step-parent.
Women were often in greater danger than men, because childbearing
was extended throughout their fertile years. Many women died in
childbirth, especially as they grew older, and, because early remarriage
was common, their children found themselves in the care of stepmoth-
ers. Court cases reveal that Hakluyt's situation was not unique, that
parents did have a tendency to favor the children of their new mar-
riages, even if that meant depriving older sons and daughters of their
rightful inheritance. The storybook theme of the wicked stepmother,

which seems so bizarre today, reflected the facts of life in Elizabethan times.

Once his inheritance was secure, Richard went to the Inns of Court, to the Middle Temple, not to study for a few months like most young landowners but to stay and live out his life as a lawyer. He was thrust into a cosmopolitan world where he became acquainted with men who were involved in the heady search for a sea passage to the Orient and ultimately became one of their leaders. Though this search never achieved success, it was important in stimulating interest in geography and navigation; it brought together scholars, merchants, many of whom had been in foreign countries, and experienced seamen. The exchange of information and ideas between these three groups, though it could not result in discovery of the nonexistent passage to the Orient, was extremely fruitful and led directly to England's later successes at sea.

The younger Hakluyt's father died when Richard was five years old, and his older namesake, who was only about twenty-five, took on the job of helping the widow and her many young children. He was apparently very conscientious in this and formed close relationships with these children, especially with the younger Richard. Young Hakluyt went to Westminster School and Christ Church College, Oxford, where he took his first degree in 1574. Looking back in 1589, he remembered visiting his cousin's chambers in the Middle Temple while on a holiday from Westminster. He noticed the map and books lying on the table and asked about them. The elder Hakluyt then pointed out to him on the map all the principal countries and landmarks and the routes of world trade. He then took him to the Bible, to Psalm 107

> where I read, that they which go down to the sea in ships, and occupy the great waters, they see the works of the Lord, and his wonders in the deep, etc. Which words of the Prophet together with my cousin's discourse (things of high and rare delight to my young nature) took in me so deep an impression that I constantly resolved, if ever I were preferred to the University, where better time, and more convenient place might be ministered for these studies, I would by God's assistance prosecute that knowledge and kind of literature, the doors whereof (after a sort) were so happily opened before me.

Historians must be ever grateful that he accomplished his goals so abundantly.

The younger Richard was ordained a minister, the only occupation for which Oxford and Cambridge trained their students. He turned to reading books of cosmography, some of which recounted recent voyages, but often combined these descriptions with passages reaching back to classical myths. He soon saw the need to supplement this reading by interviewing people who had actually been on voyages to the newly accessible parts of the world, so he increasingly spent time in London and became part of his cousin's circle. Both Richard Hakluyts were influential men whose impact on colonization was enormous; when people gathered to promote ideas for voyages to any part of the world, they were prominent in the company, and the government often sought their advice.

This was a time of great excitement. Schemes for dozens of expeditions to all parts of the world were being discussed, and interest in them was as much scientific as commercial or diplomatic. The men who came together in these gatherings had an image of England's future greatness and the exhilarating feeling that they were the people who would help make it come true. They also believed that speed was absolutely necessary, especially in establishing a firm claim to North America between the French interest on the St. Lawrence and the Spanish in the south. In 1582 the Reverend Richard Hakluyt published the first of his major works, *Divers Voyages to America,* a collection of narratives, and dedicated it to Sir Humphrey Gilbert, Raleigh's half-brother, who made his unsuccessful attempt to found a colony in Newfoundland the next year. The Hakluyts' role was to prod into action those with the resources and inclination for foreign adventures.

Hakluyt had hoped to go on this expedition himself; he never actually went to America, though he several times had hopes of doing so. His appointment as chaplain to the English ambassador in France prevented his accompanying Gilbert's 1583 expedition. The embassy post was a great opportunity for him. In Paris he mingled with scholars and seafarers just as he had in London and gained new perspectives. He also met members of the Portuguese royal family, living in exile since the disputed succession of 1580, when Philip II of Spain had imposed his rule on their country. The Portuguese had early taken the lead in the science of navigation and map-making; they had been first in the voyages of exploration. Hakluyt welcomed the chance to talk to these knowledgeable people; the pretender to the throne himself, Dom António, held discussions with him and showed him his ancient maps.

The Reverend Richard Hakluyt was back in London on leave in 1584 and became an enthusiastic backer of Raleigh's new plans. He wrote one of his most famous works, the *Discourse of Western Planting*, to convince the queen and Walsingham of the necessity of moving quickly in America. This was not intended for publication but for the private use of the court. Raleigh even kept it from being seen by some of the courtiers initially, because he thought it so convincing, and he was afraid others might try to establish a prior claim to a patent for colonization. At the same time, the elder Richard Hakluyt published a short tract on the same theme, *Inducements to the Liking of the Voyage Intended Towards Virginia.*

One thread running through the work of the younger Richard was that England needed to be more organized and rational in planning for colonization and discovery. He felt that his country would be permanently behind the leaders until it began to train people systematically for seamanship as Portugal and Spain did. He criticized the universities for sticking with the old medieval curriculum and downplaying such practical subjects as mathematics, absolutely necessary to scientific navigation. He suggested that a lectureship in navigation be set up in London and even solicited a promise from Sir Francis Drake to contribute toward its endowment.

Drake had good reason to acknowledge the need for trained mariners because he, like the Roanoke adventurers, was forced to employ Portuguese pilots on his voyages. Occasionally he recruited them by kidnapping but then was plagued by worries about their loyalty and the soundness of their navigation. Until there were adequately trained English pilots and navigators, every venture would be in the hands of men who were possibly disgruntled and sometimes dangerously treacherous. This conviction was strengthened for the younger Richard by his years in Paris and his acquaintance with the practice of other countries. He also argued strongly that to become a paying proposition, colonization would have to have genuine government sponsorship and financing. It would take many decades and many failures before that line of reasoning was generally accepted. Queen Elizabeth, despite all the informal and personal help she gave, was never willing to commit the resources of her government to foreign adventures. This aspect of his argument fell on deaf ears.

The elder Hakluyt died in 1591 when the younger was engaged in his greatest work. Roanoke's difficulties did not discourage him, but rather convinced him more than ever that he was right: a massive commitment was necessary to make colonies successful. In 1589 he published a two-volume collection of narratives entitled *The Principal Navigations, Voyages, and Traffics of the English Nation,* which was vastly enlarged and amended in a multivolume edition published between 1598 and 1600. By any standard, this is an impressive achievement. Hakluyt collected every narrative he could find; when none existed he badgered people into writing their recollections or interviewed them so he could write them himself. He scoured the country for letters written privately to friends or supporters. His standard of editing was very high; most of the changes he made were for the sake of clarity, and he strove to keep the style and intent of the original. When his work is compared to that of contemporaries who made similar compilations and often butchered their sources, the magnitude of his achievement becomes clearer. It is because of Richard Hakluyt that we know as much as we do about the early voyages and the thinking behind them.[1]

The Hakluyts shared the English obsession with undermining the Spanish empire and bringing glory to England. They saw beyond the immediate goals of the privateers, however, to the benefits that permanent colonies could bring. In their *Discourse of Western Planting* and *Inducements for the Liking of the Voyage Intended for Virginia,* written with the Roanoke ventures in mind, they laid out their arguments for genuine colonies in orderly and logical fashion. At the top of their list of goals, as for most promoters, was the pious wish to convert the Indians to the true faith. They contrasted projected English actions with the barbarous cruelty of the Spanish in Latin America, and urged the importance of bringing Protestantism to people who might otherwise be converted to Roman Catholicism.

Their strongly argued economic aims were realistically based on the idea of discovering and then developing the resources of the colonies rather than living parasitically on the Spanish treasure fleet. Their high hopes were somewhat misplaced, though, because they were based on fallacious reasoning about the relationship between climate and latitude. Because Roanoke was at the latitude of southern Spain or North Africa, the Hakluyts, along with other promoters, expected the colony to produce wine, olive oil, sugar, oranges and lemons, rice, and silk. The *Discourse of Western Planting* suggested to the queen that all these commodities would enrich the state not only indirectly but directly as a source of customs revenue.

Oil, wine, and sugar were important staples that England then bought from its actual and potential enemies around the Mediterranean Sea. Oil was particularly important, because England's chief industry, the manufacture of woolen cloth, depended on it; large amounts of oil-based soap were used in finishing the fabric. Olive oil made a sweet-smelling soap; when soap was manufactured from fish oil, the only domestic source, its strong smell could not be removed from the cloth. Being dependent on Spain and Portugal for olive oil, then, meant that these countries had a potential stranglehold on the English economy. As the elder Hakluyt said when recommending the planting of sugar canes at Roanoke, "We may receive the commodity cheaper, and not enrich infidels or our doubtful friends, of whom now we receive that commodity."

The Hakluyts were wrong about what would grow in North America because latitude is not the sole determinant of climate. Since the movement of the atmosphere in these latitudes is from west to east, weather on the east coast of North America approaches over land, whereas that of western Europe comes over water. Land absorbs and releases heat relatively quickly, so the east coast of a large continent is warm in summer and cold in winter. Since the ocean warms up slowly in the summer but retains the warmth and releases it slowly, countries along the west coast of a continent experience less extreme contrasts of temperature. The severe winter conditions in the area of Roanoke and Chesapeake Bay, comparable to those of areas much farther north in western Europe, precluded growing most of the "infinite commodities" projected by those who stayed in England. Although they were wrong about the products that would eventually flow from North American colonies, however, promoters who argued as the Hakluyts did perceived correctly that these areas would ultimately be valuable for their own products rather than simply as privateering or exploration bases.

The Hakluyts also asserted that colonies would furnish employment for the English poor. England was nearing the end of a long period of population explosion and very great inflation. Real wages continued to drop into the 1620s, and there was a widespread perception that the country was "pestered" with overpopulation, a "superfluous multitude of fruitless and idle people (here at home daily increasing)," according to one writer. Books and sermons described the social breakdown arising from the enlarged population and rising prices. The Hakluyts suggested that colonization was the answer. Not only could some of the surplus, as many as ten thousand people, be sent to the plantations, but those left at home could be employed producing necessities for the colonists and the American natives. They were sure the Indians would constitute a major market for the coarser kinds of woolen cloth, a prophecy that came true as the fur trade drained off the pelts Indians had formerly worn.

Finally, the effort required to found and sustain colonies would force England to build a truly strong navy and would give it a stock of experienced seamen, so that the country could take its rightful place as a great nation. England was experiencing a severe timber shortage at this time, with its woodlands nearing depletion; the Hakluyts pointed to the large forests and tall straight trees for masts abounding in America and recommended setting up a ship-building industry there. In the short run, before the commodities they envisioned were fully developed, an enlarged navy could support the colonization effort by fishing. An experienced and fully equipped navy would also be able to prosecute the search for a passage through America to the Pacific and the wealth of the Orient, a hope that continued to fuel exploration. The Hakluyts sometimes reminded their readers that Spain had suffered reversals and had been forced to maintain its colonists for a long time before the colonies began to pay. The thrust of all their promotional writings was that, if the effort were wholehearted and sustained, colonies in North America would similarly enrich England; but the commitment must be there consistently, and attention must be on long-range development, not immediate greed.

Hopes for such development of the Roanoke area were high when Grenville sailed back to England. He carried the news that no good harbor had yet been located, which was reinforced by the accident to the *Tiger,* but reports about the fruitfulness of the region were enthusiastic. Grenville carried a letter from Ralph Lane to Sir Francis Walsingham which said they had discovered so many rich commodities "as all the kingdoms and states of Christendom, their commodities joined in one together, do not yield either more good, or more plentiful whatsoever for public use is needful, or pleasing for delight." After exploration on the mainland, he wrote to the elder Hakluyt that it was even better: "we have discovered the main to be the goodliest soil under the cope of heaven." Grenville also affirmed, though with less hyperbole, that the land would be "most fertile."

Samples of American products, probably obtained through trade with the Indians, were sent along with the ships. A foundation, at least, for the notion that colonies could be more than privateering bases was being laid. Lane and his colonists were left behind to seek a better location with a good harbor and to conduct tests on American resources. Though Roanoke was not a good location for agricultural experimentation, Lane and his colonists had more reason to think so than would be apparent to visitors today. The island was covered with vegetation—pine, oak, cedar, sassafras, maple, holly, and dogwood trees, and undergrowth of berries, yaupon,[2] laurel, and grape vines—some of which has been destroyed by deforestation, grazing, and erosion. There was certainly reason for the inexperienced colonists to believe that the kind of agriculture they planned was possible.[3]

Lane assured Hakluyt that American commodities were not already the equal of European only because the Indians did not know how to develop them; when English technology was applied in America, "no realm in Christendom were comparable to it." This was sheer bravado on Lane's part. Though the charge to collect and experiment was taken very seriously by the specialists who were part of the expedition, the colony was dependent throughout its life on Indian aid, particularly in contributions of food.

We know little about most of the men who were left with Lane in Roanoke. A majority had probably seen military service in Ireland or on the continent. Like the Hakluyts, many English people were concerned about the effects of the unprecedented population explosion and inflation that England, along with the rest of Europe, faced. Many landowners were meeting the challenge of inflation by consolidating farmland in order to work it more efficiently, which had the effect of throwing small tenant farmers off the land and depriving them of their livelihood. Social commentators saw a crisis looming because of the many "wandering beggars" and "masterless men" thought to be roaming the countryside and congregating in the cities. To the extent that this was true, the "excess" population formed a fertile ground for recruiting colonists.

England's labor system also helped create a pool of prospective colonists. Children from all economic levels commonly left home at

the age of fourteen or fifteen; Raleigh was not at all unique in this.
The wealthy and high born sent their sons to Oxford or Cambridge or
to one of the Inns of Court, often referred to as the third university.
Well-off farmers or merchants set their sons up as apprentices, which
required the payment of a fee to the master. The sons and daughters of
the rest of the population went off to become servants: the daughters
in other people's homes, and the sons either in workshops or in hus-
bandry. This was seen as an essential part of education; even people who
could afford servants of their own sent their children into servitude.
Some scholars have pointed out that this practice neatly avoided the
problem of adolescence. The children were not free of control, because
their new masters had the same degree of power over them as a parent,
but the intense emotional conflicts of adolescence were avoided. In an
age when death was omnipresent, people of fourteen would probably
have witnessed the deaths of siblings and often parents. The wrench of
leaving home may have been lessened by the fact that many children,
like the elder Richard Hakluyt, lived with at least one step-parent and
families of half-brothers and sisters. If both parents were dead, and the
child had two step-parents, then the prospect of joining a new master
and mistress may have been welcome.

Servants generally signed annual contracts at hiring fairs, agree-
ments binding on both parties for a year. No one could decide not to
sign a contract in order to take a year off. Because the Elizabethan
poor laws made each parish responsible for the care of its own poor,
anyone found wandering the country without a contract would be
brought before the justices of the peace. To make sure their parish
would not be burdened with caring for them, the JP's would sent masterless people back to their home parishes, often with a whipping, an
event that might occur in every parish they passed through. People
normally stayed in servitude for over a decade, during which time they
accumulated enough money to set up households of their own. The
typical age at marriage was very late, over twenty-five for women, and
near thirty for men. Multigenerational households were rare, partly
because the late age at marriage usually precluded living to see your
own grandchildren, and because custom frowned on marriage before
the parties were prepared to set up their own establishment. Young
men in the midst of that long period of servitude might very well have
seen signing on to colonize in Virginia, especially when land was

promised, as an attractive opportunity. Veterans of foreign wars would have seen it as an extension of their former activities. And since Raleigh had been granted the power to impress men for his venture, some of the colonists may have gone unwillingly. An Irishman, Darby Glavin, later said that he had been forced to go against his will.[4]

It is difficult to escape the idea that, however 'these colonists were recruited, their lives were held fairly cheaply by those in command, all of whom had themselves fought in Ireland. Men of the rank and file were expendable. One of Grenville's ships, the *Lion,* which had been separated from the others on the trip over, found its supplies running short. Therefore, twenty of its company were deposited on Jamaica; only two were ever heard of again, as captives of the Spanish. Thirty-two men were set ashore on one of the islands of the Outer Banks, Croatoan, though they may have been rescued later. Ordinary people were there to serve in any way their commanders saw fit. Exploring parties regularly left boys, usually cabin boys from the ships, with Indians so that they could learn the language and act as interpreters for later colonists.

Since the men knew their interests could always be sacrificed, Ralph Lane, as governor, believed control was fundamental in his relationship with his colonists. Though none of the narratives and letters surviving from the Lane colony describe daily life there, we know that men such as Lane believed rigorous discipline was the way to deal with the representatives of the "meaner sort" who made up the rank-and-file colonists, those whom Lane referred to as "wild men of mine own nation." The fact that a jail was included in the tiny settlement indicates the importance in Lane's mind of strict control. Difficulties, even outbreaks of disease in other colonies, were explained by the breakdown of authority. Lane was proud that there was little sickness in his colony and said it was because of his "severely executed" discipline.

Disaffection must have run high, cut off as the colonists were from all alternatives. This was not uncommon; we have a great deal of evidence of such feelings from the later Jamestown colony. Nor was it confined to the English. Disgruntled Spanish colonists in the West Indies actually traded with English privateers, sometimes rigging up fake kidnappings or sieges to cover their activities. They apparently felt that the Spanish government gave all its attention to the protection of the treasure fleet and left those colonies away from its route to fend for themselves. Moreover, they often found European manufactured goods in short supply, and trading with privateers gave them a source of supplies they needed. Part of Grenville's fleet was welcomed by Spanish settlers on Puerto Rico and treated to a bullfight. Grenville repaid the welcome with a formal dinner, though neither side trusted the other.

In Roanoke it appears that the men worked willingly enough and cooperated with the discipline as long as they were exploring, especially looking for gold, or were involved in soldier-like pursuits; but isolation of the company in their compound brought trouble, which was met with stiff punishment. However successful Lane was in controlling the colonists while they were in the colony, he could not stop them from venting their feelings once back in England. Thomas Hariot, who wrote the fullest account of their year in America, said those who "slander the country" were people of "bad natures" who had been punished there for their "ill dealing." The gentlemen also complained about life in the colony, although their lot was very different from that of the lower ranks. There were about fifteen men on the venture whose titles indicate higher social status. These men, despite their rough surroundings, ate on gold and silver dishes, sometimes to a musical accompaniment. Though gentlemen did no manual labor, Lane was generous in handing out military titles to them, and he was criticized for setting up so many commanders.

Hariot, who was one of the gentlemen, thought they were too pampered and that they criticized the country unfairly once back in England, "especially if they were in company where they might not be gainsaid." Many of these big talkers had never been out of Roanoke Island, he said, and, when gold and silver were not quickly found, they wanted only "to pamper their bellies." He said they were people who had lived all their lives in cities, seeing nothing of the world.

> Because there were not to be found any English cities, nor such fair houses, nor at their own wish any of their old accustomed dainty food, nor any soft beds of down or feathers, the country was to them miserable, and their reports thereof according.

One clear lesson to be gained from this first venture was that a colony made up entirely of unattached young men and aspiring gentlemen looking for glory was sure to find trouble.

Besides the "meaner sort" and the gentlemen, there was a third category of colonists: the experts. The notes drawn up as the colony was being prepared suggested taking an engineer and a traverse-master or surveyor. Together these would be responsible for siting and supervising construction of the fort, which the instructions warned should not be too large for a small company to defend but not so small that it could not hold out against a prolonged attack. Plans called for a physician, a surgeon, and apothecaries. Physicians were academically trained, usually at the universities, and they diagnosed patients according to the theory of the four humors, which held that the basic elements, air, fire, earth, and water, were represented in the human body by blood, yellow bile or choler, phlegm, and black bile or melancholy. Sickness meant that some agent or event, such as moving from one climate to another, had unbalanced these humors. Since each environment was thought to produce a characteristic humoral balance, there was some fear that emigrants accustomed to England's even temperatures might get sick when translated to the hot climate of Carolina. The physicians' skills would thus be of prime importance in the new land. Diagnosis by a physician was a slow, philosophical process. Treatment often consisted of blood-letting, purges or enemas, and vomits, as the doctor tried to rid the body of excess or corrupted humors and restore their proper balance.

Surgeons and apothecaries were considered inferior to physicians. They were tradesmen; surgeons were often also barbers, and apothecaries were grocers who dispensed drugs and herbs along with their other products. Both learned their medicine through apprenticeship rather than formal training. Surgeons treated wounds and sores, fractures, and venereal disease; many had had experience in war. Apothecaries were expanding their scope in this period; many diagnosed illnesses in order to determine which drugs to dispense, and their care was much more affordable than that of the physicians. In fact, their interest in the new drugs coming into Europe from America and the East made them often more genuinely helpful and progressive than the physicians, who disdained the use of chemicals. The colonists' instructions specified that the surgeon would take care of wounds and treat fevers, while the physician and the apothecaries were to have the important job of gathering and testing roots and herbs for their medicinal qualities. The physician was also responsible for the general care of the soldiers. Though there were such specialists in Grenville's fleet, and some testing was done the first summer, it is doubtful that they stayed in the colony.

The notes of instruction for Lane's colony also suggested that an "alchemist" and a lapidary be sent to test minerals found in America. A German mineral specialist, Joachim Ganz, was a member of the colony, but he apparently was unreliable because he generally told those in command whatever he thought they most wanted to hear about the minerals discovered. Mining and geology, like navigation, were areas in which the English, because of their own inexperience and lack of knowledge, relied on foreign experts whom they did not trust. Ganz's eagerness to please set promoters up for a much greater disappointment when ores and specimens taken back to England proved to be worthless. Masons, carpenters, mud-wall builders, Cornish miners, and husbandmen or farmers were also seen as necessary to setting up a fort in America, though there is no evidence that rank-and-file colonists were chosen for these skills.

Finally, the notes of advice suggested sending a geographer and a painter. This was surprisingly common; the elder Hakluyt pointed out that the Spanish customarily had a painter along on voyages, as did Sir Francis Drake. Raleigh took this suggestion very seriously, showing once again that the advancement of science and learning was as important to him as greed and harassment of Spain. John White, painter, and Thomas Hariot, scientist, were sent to Roanoke with instructions to make an accurate survey and maps of the area, and to record as much as possible about the flora and fauna, the resources, and the Indians. Their collaboration produced the most remarkable record of America compiled in the early colonial period, even though it was a fraction of what they had originally intended.

Very little is known about John White before his connection with the Roanoke ventures. He evidently knew Raleigh before he went to Roanoke, and his paintings of Eskimos indicate that he probably traveled with Martin Frobisher in his search for the Northwest Passage between 1576 and 1578. The fact that Raleigh made him governor of the colony sent in 1587 indicates that he must have been a gentleman. His daughter married a craftsman, however, and it is probable that White's work as a painter brought him more in contact with the craftsmen of London than the gentry. His name is such a common one that attempts to link him with John Whites who attended Oxford or Cambridge or who appear in public records in other ways have been inconclusive. He had a married daughter in 1587, so he must have been a mature man when he went to America. The one thing we do know about him is that he was a remarkable painter, able to free himself from the artistic conventions of his time. His watercolors, beautiful in their own right, also demonstrate an extraordinary ability to see his American subjects without European preconceptions and to render them faithfully.

Thomas Hariot is now recognized as the greatest mathematician of his age. He published almost nothing during his lifetime, and many of his papers have only recently been recovered, so assessment and appreciation of his achievement have been slow in coming. He was the first person to work on binary numeration, now important in computer technology; he made the first map of the moon with a telescope he himself had built contemporaneously with Galileo's; and he did important work in number theory, linguistics, spherical trigonometry, and algebra. Over his lifetime, his interests moved from the practical work he did for Raleigh as a young man to pure science, and he was lucky enough to have patrons who made that possible.

Hariot was a young man when he went to America. He was born in Oxford in 1560 and went to St. Mary's Hall, a private institution that later affiliated with Raleigh's college, Oriel. He heard Hakluyt lecture on geography and, before his graduation in 1580, may have known Lawrence Keymis, who later collaborated with Raleigh on American ventures. Hariot joined Raleigh's household about 1582 and became central in it as Raleigh began to take over the role of his dead half-brother, Sir Humphrey Gilbert, as promoter of American colonization. Raleigh realized that the old form of navigation relying on dead reckoning was not suitable for transoceanic voyages; so Hariot lectured to Raleigh and the captains of his ships during 1583 and early 1584, teaching them the mathematics necessary to navigate using charts and instruments and to make their own charts at sea. He wrote a textbook called the *Arcticon* for these classes, but it has been lost, as has so much of his work.

This kind of lectureship was exactly what the Hakluyts had been calling for, and they praised Raleigh lavishly for taking the lead in producing educated navigators for England. Hariot and White very probably accompanied Amadas and Barlowe, who had been Hariot's pupils, on the 1584 reconnaissance voyage to Roanoke. Hariot spent the following year learning the Carolina Algonquian language from Manteo and Wanchese, the two Indians brought to England by Amadas and Barlowe, and teaching them English. By the time the 1585 venture was ready, he was able to communicate in at least a rudimentary way with the Indians they were to meet; and Manteo and Wanchese were able to function to some extent as interpreters. This breaching of the language barrier is another reason why the Hariot-White report was so remarkable.

One practical goal of their collaboration was to map the coastline of North America as an aid to future planning and voyages. White made sketches of the coastlines of some of the West Indian islands they passed. Hariot made notes and collected specimens as they traveled in Carolina, while White sketched; more intensive surveys were made when they were in a location for any length of time. The contribution of Hariot's scientific knowledge to White's skill as a painter can be seen by comparing two maps of White's. One of the coastline of North America, done by White alone, is wildly inaccurate in the latitudes assigned and draws on some conjectural sources. The map of Virginia on which the two collaborated is thought to be the most accurate American map of the sixteenth century and the first English map to be done on the basis of actual survey. In addition to immediate and practical goals, Raleigh and his servants were interested in the scientific quest to record and analyze the plants, animals, and minerals of the entire world, given new impetus by the discovery of the American continents. White's exquisite paintings of the flora and fauna of Carolina and the West Indies were an immense contribution to the science of the period.

Hariot published a book for the general reader, *A Brief and True Report of the New Found Land of Virginia,* in 1588. He and White had intended to produce a scholarly and much more elaborate natural history of Carolina, but they never did, possibly because so many of their notes and specimens were lost in the rush to leave Roanoke at the end of the first year, though Hariot said in the *Brief and True Report* that he had a much larger work nearing completion. It seems apparent that in this, as in his mathematical work, Hariot was a perfectionist who found it hard to declare his work completed and send it to the printer. In

1590 a German printer, Theodore De Bry, published Part I of his multivolume work *America*. The younger Hakluyt served as an intermediary between De Bry and Raleigh, Hariot, and White. *America*, published in Latin, French, German, and English, reprinted Hariot's *Brief
and True Report* and included woodcuts done by De Bry and his
workshop from original watercolors supplied by White, with hastily
written captions by Hariot. Hariot was immensely proud that his work
had appeared in four languages.[5]

It is ironic that White's paintings were known only through the
engravings of Theodore De Bry until the twentieth century; in fact,
they were lost during most of the intervening years. De Bry had been
faithful to the paintings in some respects but had changed them drastically in others. Whereas White's Indians are tall and slim, with long,
thin hands and feet and straight hair, the same figures were depicted by
De Bry as typical Renaissance models characterized by ringleted hair,
small chubby hands and feet, and postures pleasing to European eyes.
When White's own originals were rediscovered, the contrast between
them and the engravings was clear, and the magnitude of White's
achievement could be measured.

White is thought to have made several complete sets of watercolors
from his sketches done in America. Only his Indian paintings and the
maps were published by De Bry, and a very few of the plants and
animals appeared in herbals or natural histories. The only set of all the
paintings that remains today is a copy that was sumptuously bound for
presentation to a person whose identity is not known. These were completely lost from sight until they turned up in a bookseller's catalogue
in 1788 for fourteen guineas, a guinea being one pound plus a shilling.
The paintings were sold to the first Earl of Charlemont and taken to
Dublin, where they remained until the third earl decided to sell them
in 1865. While they were in the warehouses of Sotheby, Wilkinson,
and Hodge awaiting auction, there was a fire next door; the edges of
the book were charred, and it was water-soaked. In this condition they
were sold to a collector from Vermont who trimmed off the charring
and remounted the pictures in a new binding. There is no record of
what he did with White's original binding. These were then sold to
the British Museum, which holds them today.

In 1964, the British Museum published beautiful reproductions of
all the paintings and the copies made of them with a very informative

commentary, the first time White's own work had been faithfully and fully reproduced.[6] The watercolors from which De Bry worked have never been located, which is a loss, because they evidently contained elaborate backgrounds showing Indian life in more detail than those in the British Museum. It is ironic that we are able to know more about the work of both Hariot and White than did all but a handful of their contemporaries. Through them, we know the culture of the vanished Carolina coastal Algonquians more fully than that of many Indians whose contact with Europeans was greater and more prolonged. In ethnography and natural history, English study of North America starts from its highest point and sets a standard not reached again until modern times.

4

THE CAROLINA ALGONQUIANS
ON THE EVE OF COLONIZATION

BECAUSE of the White-Hariot collaboration and the accounts written by Barlowe and Lane, we know much more about the Indians of the Carolina Outer Banks than about most others of the time, and the culture revealed is a complex and interesting one. The southeastern Indians were in a period of transition away from old traditional patterns toward a new, more abstract and structured culture at the time they came into prolonged contact with the English. They were Algonquians, a designation that, like Sioux or Iroquois, means that all Indians in that group spoke languages with a similar basic source, just as French and Italian are Romance languages. Tribes belonging to this family of languages were numerous and widespread; the New England Indians confronted by later English colonists were also Algonquians. Within the broad grouping, each tribe spoke its own dialect.

The Carolina Algonquians lived a settled life in villages of one to two hundred people. The heart of the Indian village, like the English, was a central open space around which the houses of the most important people were ranged. There might be a palisade around these houses, but the rest of the dwellings would be out near the cornfields. Hariot thought completely unenclosed villages were "fairer" because the houses were more widely and randomly spaced. Even Lane said the land was "very well peopled and towned, though savagely." The houses were long, sometimes as much as thirty feet, and they were made of a framework of poles bent and tied to form a barrel roof. The walls and roof were of woven mats or bark, which could be rolled up to provide ventilation and light as needed. There were sleeping benches around the walls and a fire in the center, at least in winter. White's paintings clearly illustrate the towns and houses Hariot described.

These Indians were not nomadic, though hunting and gathering of roots, nuts, and shellfish were important to their winter food supply, and they lived on fishing in late winter and early spring, all of which may have involved moving away from their villages to temporary bases. The Outer Banks, too infertile for prolonged occupation, were probably short-term spring and summer fishing sites.

Agriculture was the Indians' primary food source; the fact that they could feed the colonists as well as themselves demonstrates very effectively the efficiency of their farming. White's paintings and the written descriptions of the Carolina Algonquians show them cultivating corn, beans, pumpkins, sunflowers, and an unknown herb that Hariot called *melden,* a Dutch word. They also grew gourds and a harsh form of tobacco, *Nicotiana rusticum.* The soil was prepared by both men and women, who hoed and scraped up the stubble left from the previous year, which was then gathered and burned, though the ashes were not, as Hariot thought they should have been, spread over the ground as fertilizer. The corn was planted in hills; beans and other vegetables were then planted among the hills, according to Hariot, though White painted each crop planted in rows in separate fields in the English manner. Growing beans and corn together facilitates greatly increased yields, because beans, as legumes, fix nitrogen in the soil, which continually fertilizes the corn. The Indians dug a pond for a village water supply, where that was necessary, and built a platform, illustrated by White, from which a member of the tribe constantly watched over the crops to protect them from marauding animals.

Europeans were always amazed at the tremendous yield of Indian corn compared to European grains. Barlowe said that the Americans sowed three successive crops; one put in in May was harvested in July, that sown in June was ripe in August, and the July crop was reaped in September. Hariot said an American acre produced two hundred London bushels of corn, peas, and beans, whereas forty bushels was thought a good harvest per acre in England, though he was probably over-optimistic about Indian yields.

The Carolina Algonquians prepared their food over a fire. One method was to build a grill, which Hariot called a "hurdle," of sticks and to place fish or pieces of meat on or hanging from it. Another was to make a stew, a "gallimaufrye" according to Hariot, by putting a pot filled with water over the fire and then placing meat, fish, fruits, and vegetables in it to cook. Eating maize and beans together increases the protein content of the combination by more than fifty percent because each contains the amino acids the other lacks; by cooking and eating their produce together, the Algonquians increased its nutritional quality. Hariot was very impressed with Indian cooking pots, even though they were made by coiling the clay rather than shaping it on a potter's wheel. He said that no potter in England could make larger or finer pots and that they were as durable as European brassware. When placed on the fire, they were surrounded by a ring of earth for stability. The finished food was served in wooden dishes.

Hariot described in great detail a variety of nuts, roots, and berries that Indians gathered in addition to the crops they grew. Since his job was to report on prospects for provisioning future colonists, he was most interested in the uses to which these wild foods could be put, particularly when some kind of bread was made of them. He assured his readers that the Indians hunted a great variety of beasts, fowl, and fish, which would be good for colonists as well, although they might not like to follow the natives in eating snakes or other unfamiliar foods. He said somewhat defensively that the settlers had eaten wolves or the Indians' "wolvish dogs." Hariot knew that most English people would disdain this practice, though he said there were some in the company who had tasted English dogs and reported they were nothing like these American ones. Only the most ethnocentric reader could have failed to grasp from his *Report* that English colonists would be dependent on Indian instruction in methods of hunting and preparing American game and other foods.

Possibly because their own experts did not stay on, the colonists learned less about Indian medicine than they would have liked. Hariot said the natives, like the English, used blood-letting as a cure. White painted a picture of milkweed, which the Indians called *wysauke*, probably meaning "bitter." The caption says the Indians used this herb to cure wounds caused by poisoned arrows. It actually can be used medicinally, as it is both an expectorant and a diuretic. Some thought its silk could be woven into cloth, though Hariot had a different candidate for an American silk. Colonists were pleased to find instances where native medical practices were similar to European. Hariot said the

Indians used a kind of clay, called *wapeih,* to treat sores and wounds; it was similar to the *terra Sigillata* used at home, but "more effectual." He said America had great plenty of such earths in various colors.

There were also medicines formerly unknown in Europe. The most promising was sassafras, called *winauk* by the Indians. Sassafras was thought to be the drug of choice in treating syphilis, and Hariot said it was superior to *guaiacum* or *lignum vitae* from the West Indies for that purpose. Scientific thought of this period held that nature was symmetrical. Since syphilis was thought to be a disease imported into Europe by Columbus' sailors, it was assumed that its cure would be found in America. This was part of God's care for the human race: no new evil appeared without a remedy also being offered at the same time and place. The search for a cure for syphilis was very important in the early colonies, and Hariot thought the "most pleasant and sweet smell" of Roanoke sassafras was a good indicator of its worth. He referred his readers to the work of a Spanish doctor, Nicholas Monardes, who had experimented with sassafras brought back to Seville by sailors and offered directions for its use.

Tobacco was another "sovereign remedy" according to many early promoters, and Hariot was chief among its boosters. He himself became a constant smoker and thought its use accounted for the health and strength of the Indians. Hariot described the way the Indians dried the leaves, crushed them to a powder, and then took "the fume or smoke thereof by sucking it through pipes made of clay," and he said the colonists "used to suck it after their manner."

The medicinal effect of tobacco was supposed to result from its action in opening the body's pores and allowing the elimination of "gross humors." Since the balance of the four humors was all-important in contemporary medical thinking, disease was thought to be caused by an oversupply of one or more humors. If the body could not eliminate them, they might become corrupt or foul and cause disease. This is why so much of medicine focused on bleeding, emetics, and purges of various sorts—a preoccupation not totally different from concern over constipation today. Hariot wrote that tobacco opened "all the pores and passages of the body" and that he and his comrades had seen "many rare and wonderful experiments of the virtues thereof." Unfortunately, Hariot's was the first documented case of a constant smoker who died of cancer; his was located in his nose.

The most striking result of the White-Hariot collaboration was the portraits of Indian life. White's Indians are tall, strong, dignified figures. He did several portraits of leading men and women, and his effectiveness was such that these people live for us today in a way that much more completely documented tribes do not. White's pictures show the Indians wearing skins, with different styles of dress according to age, sex, and office.

Hariot, like many observers, commented on the modesty of Indian women. Women wore their hair long or tied up. Many of the adults wore jewelry and various decorations; some of the decorations may have been painted on, others, especially the women's, may have been tattoos meant to represent necklaces, headbands, and bracelets. Hair style, dress, and tattooing indicated a woman's village or tribe. One picture shows a mother carrying a young child on her back; she has no cradleboard, rather the baby's leg is thrust through one of her bent arms and its arms are around her neck. He shows a child with a pad of moss covering her genitals tied with a cord around her waist; Hariot's notes say that children adopt adult dress at the age of ten. We are offered a personal insight into the cultural confrontation going on around them: the child is carrying a small English doll.

The men generally had their heads shaved except for a roach in the middle and, sometimes, a short fringe in front; some had it longer and tied. Only the old men let their beards grow. Some men wore strips of leather as earrings. Important men wore breastplates or gorgets of copper, obtained in trade from as far away as Lake Superior. Apparently their body paint indicated their village or tribe as well as rank; marks of rank were inscribed on the backs of their shoulder-blades. Special clothes and decorations were worn for ceremonial purposes; Hariot said they painted for war "in the most terrible manner that they can devise." One whom Hariot called the "conjuror," a medicine man, wore a flattened woodpecker on the side of his head as a badge of office. The skin he wore had the face of the animal hanging down in front. Some other men wore feathers in their hair.

White allowed his Indians to speak for their own culture; their faces are dignified and self-sufficient. He did not pose or manipulate them, so they are represented in postures and attitudes that would have seemed foreign and even ungainly to European eyes. We see them preparing food and eating it, fishing, tending their fields, performing their religious ceremonies; it is an incomparable record.

The English audience would have approved much about the Indian culture White and Hariot described, particularly the regulation of each person's position in the society by public marks. English citizens in Elizabethan times showed by their clothing and hairstyle, as well as special badges, their place of origin, occupation, and marital and social status. They expected to be able to tell at a glance the positions of the people with whom they dealt. These public marks were also meant to keep categories stable, to prevent people from sliding over into a status they did not deserve. Special laws, called sumptuary laws, regulated the amount and value of lace and other decorations one could wear according to one's rank in society; punishments fell on those who tried to dress above their station. That Indian culture also regulated relationships and status in this way made it worthier of respect, more recognizable as a real society.

When Hariot and White described the Indians' political and social organization, their main goal was to indicate how it would adjust to the English presence and whether it could be subject to manipulation. Despite this utilitarian aim and the ethnocentric lens through which they viewed Indian culture, though, we can learn a great deal from them about how that society functioned. Modern authorities believe that the Indian societies of the Southeast were moving in the direction of true statehood and away from the earlier system of very loosely connected chieftaincies, each controlling a single village or band. Since this line of development was interrupted by the coming of the Europeans, we will never know what those states would have looked like.

Hariot said the chiefs, called *werowances,* controlled between one and eighteen towns, and many controlled six or eight. The greatest were able to muster seven or eight hundred fighting men. Chiefs wore special jewelry and decorations and had extra privileges, especially in trading contacts with the English. Barlowe marveled at the great awe in which these *werowances* were held; "no people in the world carry more respect to their King, Nobility, and Governors, than these do." This was high praise, for stability, marked by acceptance of one's place in the social order, was important in the time of Queen Elizabeth. Many feared that England was losing just that quality, because with inflation and the new capitalist emphasis new men were rising and others were falling in wealth, a process that strained the old order.

Colonists were not sure that *werowance* was the equivalent of chief or king; they reported that the Indians called all English commanders *werowances*. Some of the chiefs with whom the settlers dealt seemed to be able to command action on the part of others, though this may have been one effect of the introduction of European trade goods among them. Those Indians in contact with the English developed advantages over other tribes as they came to control the flow of European goods. The coming of the Europeans clearly upset relationships in several ways. There was dissension within and between tribes over whether the Indians should cooperate with the English to ensure the supply of trade goods or resist their encroachment. Some tribes were weakened by this split; others were strengthened as weaker units came under their protective alliance.

Carolina Algonquian society was stratified, with an elite family or clan at the top. This "aristocracy" was probably interrelated from tribe to tribe, and alliances may have been forged on the basis of such family relationships rather than through an abstract political process. Chiefs of large and important tribes may have placed close relatives in other villages as observers or advisors. When joint action was deemed necessary, then, a means of cooperation was already in existence.

The chief and his family were held in great awe and moved among their people in state, but the extent of the *werowances'* actual political power is unclear. Southeastern Indians typically made decisions through a process of discussion designed to arrive at a consensus. Chiefs did not have coercive power, and their leading role was shared with a council. They had to convince their followers that a course of action was wise rather than command it. Theirs was a redistributive kingship. Much of the tribe's material wealth flowed into the hands of the chief, but his role was to spread those goods among the people. The chief's status and power derived from his redistributive function; the term *werowance* actually means "he who is rich." Though the "royal family" wore special clothes and jewelry and were treated with great respect, there is no indication that they lived differently from the rank and file; and a chief who attempted to engross those goods he should have passed on would have lost his people's respect.

The system of justice among southeastern Indians was different from that the English knew. Its goal was to maintain an equilibrium in which peace would be constant; injuries were avenged in kind in the

interests of this equilibrium. Hariot wrote that there were formal punishments for some crimes, mentioning particularly theft and
whoremongering, and that these could range from beating or forfeiture
to death, depending on the "greatness of the facts." Usually, though,
punishments within and between tribes were matters for informal
vengeance carried out by the victim's clan, family, or tribe. Punishment is really the wrong word, because there was no concept of
retribution upon a responsible individual. Rather, the perpetrator of
the harm was liable, along with his entire clan or tribe, for restitution
whether the act was intentional or accidental. Those avenging a deed
would seek to inflict exactly the same harm on someone of the
perpetrator's clan or tribe. It would make no difference if that injury
came to the actual person involved as long as equilibrium was restored.
Once that was accomplished, both sides could live peacefully.

Despite Barlowe's assertion that wars among the Carolina Algonquians were "very cruel and bloody," and the population wasted by war
and civil dissension, most modern authorities agree that Indian warfare
was much more limited than European, since it was not conducted
with the goal of conquest and, once the need for vengeance was
satisfied, did not lead to further conflict. Hariot's description of Indian
warfare may have been closer to the truth; he characterized it as conducted mostly by surprise raids: "set battles are very rare." It was not
recognizable to the Europeans as subject to the same rules as their
wars, and could therefore be seen as disorderly.

Equilibrium also involved reciprocity in bestowing favors. Barlowe
and Amadas experienced this almost immediately. A few days after
their anchorage at Roanoke, three Indians appeared. One approached
their ships and stood on a point of land opposite. Several of the
expedition's leading men rowed over to him while he waited, "never
making any show of fear or doubt." He spoke to them "of many things
not understood by us," then accompanied them on board one of the
ships, willingly, as Barlowe was at pains to stress. The explorers gave
him a hat and shirt and other things and let him taste English wine
and meat, which he seemed to like. After looking over both their
ships, he went back to his own canoe, and they saw him fishing not far
off. Barlowe says he fished about half an hour and, when his boat was
fully loaded, he came back to the English ships, divided the fish into
two piles, and gestured with his hands to indicate that one pile of fish

should go to each ship. He was unwilling to depart until he had reciprocated the English hospitality and restored the balance between them, a major social obligation in his culture.

Thomas Hariot's most important task was to study native culture, and nothing about the Indians fascinated him so much as their religion. Here his work with Manteo and Wanchese paid off, because he was able to discuss religion, Christian and Indian, in remarkable depth with the people he met. Most reports concentrated on ceremonies and regalia, the most accessible aspects of Indian religion. Arthur Barlowe, lacking Hariot's ability to discuss beliefs, reported that the Indians worshiped an idol, which he called a "mere illusion of the Devil." He compared its use as an oracle in wartime to the ancient Roman practice of consulting Apollo. White painted a picture of this idol, called *Kiwasa,* placed to watch over the bodies of dead chiefs. Hariot's notes said that the idol was about four feet tall, with a white breast and flesh-colored face; all the rest was black, except for white spots on the thighs. It wore a chain of white beads and copper, the Indians' most highly esteemed decoration.

Several of John White's paintings depicted religious ceremonies, all celebrating the agricultural cycle and its products. These rites indicated a highly organized religion appropriate to a farming culture, one that Hariot took very seriously. He wrote that the Indians considered tobacco so precious that they used it in their worship, thinking "their gods are marvelously delighted therewith." Sometimes they made a "hallowed fire" and cast tobacco into it. At other times, especially when they were in danger or dedicating a new structure such as a fish weir, they threw it up into the air. These sacrifices were accompanied by "strange gestures, stamping, sometimes dancing, clapping of hands, holding up of hands, and staring up into the heavens, uttering therewithal and chattering strange words and noises."

One of White's most interesting paintings, labeled "their high feasts," shows a large festival. According to Hariot, Indians came from all the surrounding towns to participate, each specially attired. The painting shows Indians dancing around a circle of carved posts, which Hariot compared to sculptures of nuns wearing veils. The dance went on continuously for a long period, with participants dropping out to rest and later rejoining it. A second painting shows Indians sitting around a fire, praying, according to the caption. Hariot said that this

ceremony took place after the dancing ended but might also be held
after any escape from danger. It may represent the "hallowed fire" he
described earlier. In this ceremony, the worshipers had rattles made of
gourds dried and hollowed out with stones placed in them. He
described their singing as "making merry."

This "high feast" may have been the Green Corn ceremony, celebrated throughout the Southeast when the late corn crop was ripe,
probably in late July or early August. This, the major ceremonial event
of the southeastern Indians' religious calendar, involved the purging of
all evil and old quarrels and purification for the new year. Fires were
extinguished because they had become corrupted by human inadequacy
over the past year. New, pure sacred fires were kindled on every
hearth. All sources of friction between people were to be extinguished
also, and enemies were reconciled to each other. For many Indians, the
ceremony began with fasting and even purges, followed by feasting and
gaiety. It combined the functions of a thanksgiving and a new year's
feast, acknowledging divine care and renewing a sense of purpose for
the coming year.

Hariot wrote in greater detail about Indian theology than about any
other single subject. He said that the Indians believed there are many
gods, collectively called *Mantoac,* which may be a variant of the more
familiar *Manitou.* One chief god had existed from all eternity; the others were "of different sorts and degrees." When the chief god created
the world, he first made the other deities "to be as means and instruments to be used in the creation and government to follow." The sun,
moon, and stars were such "petty gods." This god first made the water
and the other gods then made all creatures, visible and invisible. A
woman was the first human being, and she conceived children by one of
the deities. Hariot said that the Indians had no idea how long ago all
this had taken place, as they had no way of keeping records, "but only
tradition from father to son." Their gods were all represented in human
shape; individually these images were called *Kiwasa,* collectively
Kiwasowak. They were placed in buildings Hariot referred to as tem-
ples, called *machicomuck.* In White's painting of a village, the temple
is the largest building.

Hariot said the Indians believed in the immortality of the soul and
that when the soul is separated from the body by death, it goes either

to heaven to live with the gods, "there to enjoy perpetual bliss and happiness," or to a place near the setting sun called *Popogusso* to burn continually in a great pit. Its destination depended on behavior on earth. The Indians knew about the fate of human souls because of two near-death experiences that had occurred recently. In one, which had taken place a few years before the English came, a "wicked man" had died and been buried. The next day they saw the earth over his grave move and uncovered him. He told them that his soul had been about to enter *Popogusso* when one of the gods saved him and gave him permission to return to teach his people how to avoid "that terrible place of torment."

The other out-of-body experience occurred while the English were actually there, but in a town sixty miles away. It was similar in that a dead and buried man was taken out of the grave. While he was dead his soul had remained alive and had traveled on a "long broad way," along which grew "rare and excellent fruits" even beyond his powers to describe. Finally he came to a town of handsome houses where he met his long-dead father, who urged him to return to show his friends how to be good so they could enjoy "the pleasures of that place." He was promised that once this was done he would be able to return there.

Chief men were not buried like ordinary Indians. They were cut open and the inner organs removed, after which the skin was pulled back and the flesh cut and scraped from the bones. The flesh and organs were dried in the sun and then enclosed in mats. The bones, still held together by the ligaments, were also dried and then covered with leather to simulate flesh. Finally the skin was restored over all to give the appearance of the body as it was. These bodies were laid on a high deck side by side in a special temple, with the mats containing their dried flesh at their feet. A *kiwasa* and a priest were set to watch over the chiefs' corpses. Ralph Lane wrote that the Indians had a monthly ceremony to commemorate great men's deaths.

Twice in his book Hariot made remarks about the political uses to which the Indians put religion. The concept of heaven and hell was used, he said, to make the common people respect their leaders and take great care to obey their wishes in order to escape punishment after death. In his note to White's painting describing the treatment of chiefs' corpses, he wrote, "These poor people are thus instructed by nature to reverence their princes even after death." Hariot knew very

well that the same could be said of England, and his later life was troubled because he was repeatedly suspected of just such subversive opinions.

Hariot and White distinguished between priests and conjurors, who
wore different clothes and badges of office and functioned quite
differently. The priest White painted was an old man, and Hariot
described priests as usually "well stricken in years," with more than
common experience. The priests, chosen for their knowledge and wisdom, were leaders of the organized religion whose theology Hariot
described. They superintended the relationship to the gods that caused
the crops to grow and the fields to be fruitful and were responsible for
keeping the people in the proper path and placating the deities; thus
they constituted the link between the gods and the people necessary in
an agricultural society.

The conjuror, a much younger man, wore a woodpecker in his hair
and an animal face on his breechclout to indicate his office. He was
linked to the older, individualistic hunting cult, and his role was magical. Whereas the priest attained his office by his wisdom and
experience, the conjuror, "the flyer" as White called him, was selected
because he was seen as having magical powers, probably derived from a
personal connection with a supernatural being. The bird he wore indicated his connection to the upper world where the gods live. The face
on his reddish animal pelt, if it was a foxskin, signified that he was
capable of curing snakebite, because the fox kills and eats snakes.
Since disease was principally thought to be caused by the spirits of
vengeful animals who had been killed improperly, the conjuror, with
his magical connections to the animal world, would have been prominent in healing the sick, probably with a combination of charms and
herbal medicine. He would therefore have been an important man in
the community. Both men were described by Hariot as able magicians,
and he wrote that people put great stock in what the conjuror said
because it so often turned out to be true. Lane also said the people
spoke "incredible things" of the powers of *kiwasa*.[1]

A late sixteenth-century English audience would not have found
these descriptions foreign to their experience because belief in magic
was widespread in England. Virtually every parish had a magical prac-
titioner, a "cunning man" or "wise woman" who used a combination
of herbal medicine and charms to effect cures, just as the Indian sha-

mans did. Moreover, the combination of religious and magical functions was also seen in England; often the parish priest doubled as the
"cunning man."

English people and Indians alike believed that the world was popu-
lated by a myriad of supernatural beings who existed with the permission of God and the devil, and that some human beings were able to
align themselves with these powers and therefore had extraordinary
abilities to cure or to foretell the future. These powers could be used
for good or ill, and, in both societies, people thought to have them
were feared and sometimes hated. Witchcraft prosecutions, common in
sixteenth- and seventeenth-century England, were one manifestation of
this combination of feelings. On the other hand, many people consulted such magical practitioners when they felt they could not cope
with their own situations, and the most effective among them had great
reputations. In this respect as in others, Indian culture did not seem so
foreign to early English colonists as we might expect. In fact, in later
colonies settlers sometimes consulted Indian medicine men when they
had stubborn medical problems.[2]

Some colonists found Indian culture not only interesting, but also
praiseworthy. Here the distinction between a man like Hariot, who
really studied the Indians around him, and others who simply repeated
their preconceptions is very striking. Ralph Lane, for example, said
the land was poor in comparison with what it could be under English
care, because the Indians did not know how to use the resources they
had. Grenville said the land had never been "labored with man's
hand," an early example of the "virgin land" myth. John Gerard was
the author of a very famous herbal, a guide to the plants of the world;
he invested in some of the Roanoke ventures and was interested in
their scientific discoveries, though he never left England. In his
description of milkweed, he stressed that it was potentially a source of
very fine silk, and went on,

> This considered; behold the justice of God, that as he hath shut up
> those people and nations in infidelity and nakedness; so he hath not as
> yet given them understanding to cover their nakedness, nor matter
> wherewith to do the same; notwithstanding the earth is covered with
> this silk, which daily they tread under their feet, which were sufficient
> to apparel many kingdoms if they were carefully manured, and cher-
> ished.

Those with little knowledge simply assumed the inferiority of Indian culture.

Hariot, on the other hand, stressed the ingenuity and mastery demonstrated in Indian adaptation to the environment. The single most impressive item of native manufacture was the dugout canoe, which both Hariot and Barlowe considered a marvel. Each man included a long description of the Indians' alternately burning and scraping out the inside of a giant tree to make boats capable of carrying twenty men. Hariot began his description: "The manner of making their boats in Virginia is very wonderful." Canoes were much better adapted to the American environment than bulky and cumbersome European boats because they could maneuver in the rocky and swift-flowing streams; if an impassable stretch appeared, the Indians simply picked up the canoe and went around it, whereas the Europeans were stymied.

White also rejected the idea that the Indians were far inferior to Europeans, and he found a very interesting way to suggest that the Indians were not so alien as those in England might think. He followed his Indian portraits with reconstructions of the ancestors of the English nation, the Picts and Britons. These figures are in many ways reminiscent of his portrayals of the Carolina Algonquians: they are painted all over, the Picts with decorations and the British solid blue. Their clothing resembles Indian dress. The notes say that Pictish and British women were as warlike as their men, and the introduction to the series points out that the English were once as savage as the Indians. Cultural differences, not a permanent racial gulf, separated Europeans and Indians.

Beyond the ingenuity of the Indians were more fundamental qualities that thoughtful Europeans admired. Indians, who held tribal wealth in common, seemed to practice Christian virtues more than the Christians did. After the earliest contacts with the Carolina Algonquians, Barlowe wrote that "a more kind and loving people, there cannot be found in the world." He stressed that they always kept their promises. Hariot was especially impressed with the Indians' generosity and lack of covetousness; they were not obsessed with accumulation of wealth but content with what they had, living in friendship with their neighbors. They were not greedy, even in eating. Hariot said their sobriety and restraint in eating and drinking contributed to their long lives "because they do not oppress nature." In another place, he wrote with great feeling: "I would to God we would follow their example. For we should be free from many kinds of diseases which we fall into by sumptuous and unseasonable banquets, continually devising new sauces, and provocation of gluttony to satisfy our unsatiable appetite." Hariot and Barlowe both admired the orderliness and restraint of Indian society, Barlowe saying that the Americans were "as mannerly, and civil, as any of Europe." Even Ralph Lane described them as "naturally most courteous."

Praise for Indian generosity, lack of covetousness, and contentment with their lot was significant. English people of the late sixteenth century believed they lived in a disintegrating society; the capitalism that made colonization possible also broke down the old sense of community. It was commonly believed that in former times England had been a country of tightly knit village communities in which each person had an important position with recognized rights and responsibilities. The lord or gentleman had great privileges, but in return he cared for those who could not care for themselves, the old, poor, and sick. In this mythical past, neighbors helped each other; every person, no matter how humble, counted in the village structure. Now competition was replacing cooperation, and many people were being cut out altogether. As efficiency became a goal in agriculture, old ways involving large labor forces of tenant farmers were giving way to rationalized field systems. A frequent theme of the Hakluyts was the large number of "wandering poor" in England, people who were losers in the drive for efficiency, and they hoped colonization would be one answer to this problem; England's excess population could be poured into America.

Capitalist ventures also meant that the old social hierarchy was no longer stable. Some people were rising and others were falling, and this was universally decried. Early modern Europeans did not think of change as development and therefore normal; they were afraid that such instability would inevitably lead to total lack of order, that society was developing centrifugal forces that would ultimately tear it apart. Despite the fact that those connected with Roanoke were intimately involved in capitalist ventures and that their goal was to make a large amount of money, they were frightened of the England they saw evolving around them and longed nostalgically for the simpler, more comfortable relationships they thought had characterized the country in the past. Barlowe and Hariot were actually saying the Indians exhibited qualities the English formerly had but had lost, qualities they wished their society still held.

All English people, no matter how sympathetic to Indian culture, of course believed their own culture was superior. All were ultimately ethnocentric. Because it was Christian they felt that the culture they brought to America could not have an equal in the world. No relativism was possible; Christianity was true religion, all other beliefs were false. They also assumed that their technology was necessarily better than anything the Indians had to offer. They were disturbed by their own inability to measure up to the Christian virtues of sharing and lovingkindness as well as the Indians did, but this could not erase their sense of doctrinal and intellectual superiority. Early English colonists in America, including those at Roanoke, believed it would be a simple matter to convert the Indians to Christianity and European civilization. The Indians' very intelligence would facilitate their conversion because they would recognize European culture as better and would naturally be eager to become assimilated to it.

Indians on the Outer Banks were not without experience of Europeans. Barlowe reported that they had some metal tools salvaged from a shipwreck some twenty years before in which all the sailors had died. Six years before that, some Europeans had emerged from a shipwreck alive and had stayed with the Carolina Algonquians for about three weeks. They lashed two canoes together, rigged a sail from their shirts, and sailed off with all the food they could carry. No one knew what became of them, but the Indians later found their boats cast away and assumed that they had been shipwrecked a second time.

Despite the Americans' previous acquaintance with Europeans, however, the colonists reported that the Indians esteemed them as gods, and that they were ripe for conversion. Hariot believed the natives' religion, inadequate though he thought it was, would prepare their minds to receive true religion. Just as they were impressed with English technology, he thought they would see the superiority of Christianity over their own faith. They were amazed by Hariot's scientific instruments, which he said so far exceeded their ability to understand, much less to manufacture, that they thought the colonists "specially loved" by God. The superhuman status of the English was enhanced by their apparent ability to get along without women, since no English women accompanied this colony, and, according to Hariot, the colonists were not interested in the Indian women as sexual partners.

Hariot preached to the inhabitants of every village he traveled through and lamented that his command of Carolina Algonquian was not better so he could do more. He told them of the contents of the Bible, that it was the only word of God, and described God's works and the way to salvation through Christ, "with many particularities of Miracles and chief points of religion, as I was able then to utter, and thought fit for the time." He was distressed that many of the people attached special significance to the book itself as a kind of medicine bundle with magical power and wanted to stroke it or rub their bodies with it. He affirmed several times that the Indians were very desirous to be made Christians. When the English knelt to pray, the Indians imitated them by kneeling and moving their lips also: "Wherefore that is very like that they might easily be brought to the knowledge of the gospel. God of his mercy grant them this grace."

If the Indians thought of the settlers as gods, it may have been due to the different susceptibility of the two populations to disease. The impact of European diseases on American Indians is one of the most tragic aspects of the story of the early colonies. The physical impact was devastating; psychologically the effect was almost as bad. In order to understand this problem, it is necessary to go back to the beginnings of Indian habitation of the American continents. The ancestors of the present-day Native Americans were from the continent of Asia. They traveled to America during the last Ice Age, when the Bering Strait was dry land because so much of the earth's water was tied up in ice that the sea level was much lower than it is today. These people were nomadic hunters following the big game of the day, woolly mammoths and mastodons, and they moved as the animals moved; their migration from one continent to another was not intentional. The period of glaciation extended from 40,000 to 10,000 years ago. At the end of the period, the land bridge became a strait and migration was cut off.

From that time forward, the Indians developed in isolation, which meant they were not exposed to the diseases rampant in the rest of the world. Plague and smallpox were big killers in Europe, and typhus and typhoid were common. Infant mortality rates were extremely high in England, but those who survived to adulthood generally had a degree of immunity to the endemic diseases except in those epidemic years when the pathogens mutated and devastated the population. The young men sent to the colonies were in the stage of life when they were most able to resist disease. The Indians lacked acquired immunity to all the diseases endemic in Europe; plague and smallpox killed many and others died of influenza or measles. It was not uncommon for an entire village to be wiped out when one of these struck. Demographers estimate that up to 90 percent of the native population along the east coast of North America may have been destroyed by disease during the first century of contact.

These physical facts are horrifying; the psychological ramifications of the realization that whereas the Indians died in droves the English were rarely touched are almost unimaginable. What made it worse was that, because Indians would flee the epidemics, the diseases broke out in places the English had never been. It looked as if the colonists could strike by remote control. Lane reported the native belief that the settlers were spirits risen from the dead and therefore more powerful than humans, and they pointed to an outbreak of sickness in the night one hundred miles away in which many died. Hariot reported a similar belief, though he thought the diseases appeared only in villages that had planned some evil stroke against the colonists. When the English departed from such a town, the disease would break out within a few days, with reported mortality figures of from twenty to one hundred twenty, which were enormous for that population. The elders reported nothing of the kind had ever happened before.

The Indians came to the conclusion that it was the work of the English god, killing those who were enemies to his people. Hariot said they thought the colonists were "not born of women, and therefore not mortal," but risen spirits, some of whom had taken on human shape, while others were still invisible. These not-yet-incarnate spirits fired invisible bullets that struck people with disease. Other Indians thought the colonists could fire their guns in Roanoke and cause disease to strike anywhere. Especially striking about Hariot's report is that he himself, though the most sophisticated thinker on the expedition, was puzzled by the strange distribution of deaths. He was inclined to think that it was somehow the work of God and that it might be related to a comet and an eclipse of the sun that had occurred while they were at Roanoke. His belief that calamity visited only those villages where the Indians had planned some harm to the English made God's striking them seem not wanton and random, but reasonable. At the end of the discussion, Hariot said he was still puzzled.

Indians differed among themselves as to whether they should defy the invading Europeans or attempt to live peacefully with them. One strategy employed by Indians facing the apparent superiority of the English and their god was to attempt to align themselves with the new power in their midst. They sent to the English to ask them to pray for the *werowance* nearest the settlement when he was sick, and they asked for prayers when there was a drought in the early summer of 1586. They also asked that the English god should punish some of their enemies, alleging that they had plotted against the colonists. Hariot scolded those who made this request, telling them that God did not subject himself to human requests but only to his own "good pleasure." His people properly prayed only that events should accord with the divine will and wisdom. As it happened, disease did break out among the enemy Indians and those who had made the request came to the English to thank them for carrying out their requests so well. That particular lesson backfired.

The English knew that they were not gods and were aware of their own vulnerability. Nevertheless, they affirmed they could control their relationship with the Indians. Hariot wrote that the Indians were "not to be feared": their weapons were bows and arrows and truncheons and their armor was made of "sticks wickered together with thread." He said they frequently ran from the English, who were superior in their discipline as well as their weapons. Lane wrote with typical bravado that "ten of us with our arms prepared, were a terror to a hundred of the best sort of them." Barlowe had earlier reported that English guns caused the Indians to tremble with fear, and their weapons, clubs and arrows headed with animal teeth or stag horns, were inferior.

Guns were terrifying, partly because of the smoke and noise they made, and partly because the wounds they caused were so dirty and nasty. On the other hand, it is not clear that, in guerrilla warfare situations, all the advantages would be on the English side. The colonists' guns were matchlock muskets, which meant that they lacked rifling on the interior of the barrel and were therefore very inaccurate. Soldiers had to carry a lighted wick or match at all times in order to ignite the powder in the firing chamber; in wet weather they could be in very real trouble. The matchlock was slow to load; the most skilled could load two balls a minute. A skilled bowman could silently shoot up to twelve arrows a minute, with greater accuracy and a similar range. The military expert who advised Raleigh suggested that a very large number of bowmen be sent with the expedition, as did the elder Richard Hakluyt, who pointed to the danger of losing the entire supply of gunpowder by an explosion. The one great advantage of muskets over bows was that the latter required skill, and England no longer had the intensive training in martial arts that would have made bows and arrows feasible as weapons for the colonists. John White complained about the difficulty of fighting the Indians dispersed among the trees instead of massed as a European army would be; the matchlock's inaccuracy multiplied these problems.

Whatever the actual military balance between the two groups, there was a much more fundamental war the Indians could wage, one before which the English were relatively helpless. Lane wrote of the Indians' making war by withdrawing from contact with them, underlining the fact that, most of the time, the colonists were totally dependent on the Indians for food. The Indians planted crops for them and built weirs to catch fish. Hariot said of the weirs, "There was never seen among us so cunning a way to take fish withall." He also made it clear that the colonists ate what the Indians ate during their stay in America.

As long as relations remained good between the two groups, the colonists were well fed. When relations became strained, their vulnerability was acute. Lane wrote that in March, 1586, there had been an unfulfilled plan to withdraw from contact with the English. Had this happened,

> there had been no possibility in common reason (but by the immediate hand of God) that we could have been preserved from starving out of hand. For at that time we had no weirs for fish, neither could our men skill of the making of them, neither had we one grain of corn for seed to put into the ground.

When a similar plan was later carried out by neighboring Indians, including the breaking up of the weirs made for the English, Lane was forced to disperse his colony in small parties to live off the land, a strategy that made all of them relatively helpless before any type of attack.

Exaggerated feelings of superiority and actual vulnerability are a very dangerous combination. Because of their conflicting goals and the background of the men chosen as colonists, the English were ill-prepared to carry out a consistent program toward the Indians or to build a colony. The actual course of policy development and the unfolding relationships within the colony and with the Indians will be examined in the next chapter.

5

THE STRAINED RELATIONSHIP
OF INDIANS AND COLONISTS

As plans were being made for the Lane colony, all involved agreed that good treatment of the Indians was essential. The Spanish example in Latin America, whose iniquities were magnified in English retelling, was held in horror, and promoters felt strongly that Protestant Englishmen could not act as the Spanish had done. The notes drawn up for the direction of planners suggested a series of punishments for any colonist who violated an Indian's rights. For rape of an Indian woman the punishment was to be death; for forcing Indian labor, three months' imprisonment. Striking or misusing an Indian would result in twenty blows with a cudgel in the presence of the Indian and, for entering a native's house without his permission, the penalty was six months' imprisonment "or slavery." Clearly, officials in England were intent on establishing a just relationship. Hariot, in America, also believed it was absolutely necessary to win the Indians' favor rather than impose English ways on them.

The elder Hakluyt pointed out that gentleness was simply good policy. If the colonists sought revenge for every slight, then the Indians could destroy all their crops and trade, "and so the English nation there planted and to be planted, shall be rooted out with sword and hunger." The inability of English colonists to cope with the environment and achieve self-sufficiency made them too vulnerable for a swaggering policy. Moreover, Hakluyt knew that conquest for its own sake was pointless because the colonies had to become paying propositions if they were to continue; commercial success would come only through the kind of knowledge of the country and its resources that the Algonquians alone could give. To alienate them meant danger in the short run and failure in the long run. Though they never saw America, the Hakluyts had advanced far beyond the arrogant assumption of Indian ignorance voiced by men like Lane and Grenville.

In choosing colonists, rank and file as well as commanders, however, promoters made it virtually certain that their good intentions would be violated. Sir Richard Grenville and Ralph Lane had served in the bitter and cruel Irish campaigns, and many of the colonists were soldiers. They knew very well the correct way to deal with an alien population on whom they were intruding and before whom they were vulnerable. Their Irish experience had convinced them that Hakluyt's "forbearing of revenge" was bad policy. Invading Europeans should rather avenge every slight or challenge to their authority, regardless of how insignificant, so that the natives would not think of them as weak or irresolute. Such was the practice in Ireland, where terror had become official policy.

Ireland was the site of the first Elizabethan experiments in colonization. In the 1560s and 1570s, the English government began a concerted effort to extend its control over the entire island, and soldiers and colonists were sent to accomplish this goal. The colonies were organized in much the same way as later American plantations: planters, given estates and patents for colonization, brought over large numbers of settlers. It had become important to re-establish English power in Ireland because Elizabeth and her councillors feared its use as a base from which Spain or France could attack. A strong English presence was deemed particularly crucial in the Gaelic areas of Ulster and Munster, especially as Munster was just across from England's important western ports. England's claims in Ireland derived from its conquest by the Normans in the twelfth and thirteenth centuries; the sixteenth-century invasion was justified by pointing to the supposed "savage" state of the Irish people, who were portrayed as pagans and sometimes even as cannibals. Their practice of moving their flocks seasonally served as an excuse to call them nomads, implying that they did not really farm the land, had not made it theirs by mixing their labor with it.

Assertions that the Irish were significantly lower on the scale of human development than the English allowed the invaders to use tactics that would have been unacceptable at home. It was assumed that the savage condition always involved tyranny over the general population by a small number of men, so the invaders could see themselves as offering liberation. When they met resistance, the English intensified their military activities until finally there was a full-blown policy of terror and attrition in Munster under Sir Humphrey Gilbert, Raleigh's half-brother. His was a total war; no distinction of persons, ages, or sexes was made, and he avowed that, in killing women and children as well as men of military age, his goal was to starve out the rebels. Those who approached his tent walked up a path lined with severed heads, whose grisly object was to instill fear. When opponents capitulated, he demanded the most humiliating obeisance from them. Resistance was used as justification for English expropriation of rebel lands, which were regranted to English gentlemen, who then brought over numbers of settlers to work them and maintain the English presence. Many of these gentlemen were from the west of England, and Raleigh and Grenville were prominent among them.

The rank and file, soldiers and colonists, learned different lessons in Ireland. Those who could be encouraged to come were rarely successful farmers in their own country; rather they were marginal people, the vagabonds and beggars who worried so many in England. These found that the relative lack of control over their activities gave them opportunities for pillage of the local people, and made disruptive and even mutinous activities possible. Frequently they lacked a highly developed sense of loyalty to their commanders and mission and many deserted to the enemy, the Gaelic Irish. Neither the commanders nor their soldiers, with the lessons of Ireland in their minds, were good choices to carry English culture and religion to the natives of America, or even to replicate English society there.[1]

Why were such people sent to America? The answer lies in the fact that promoters were divided in their own minds about how to approach the American natives. They sincerely believed that the Indians would be won over by a pacific approach; the natives' very intelligence would make them desire instruction in English ways. But the colonists could not place their trust in that belief because of contemporary ideas about human nature. Relationships between people were seen as always potentially involving conflict and treachery. Keeping your guard up was universally necessary, whether you were dealing with English people, other Europeans, or American natives. As a propagandist for the later Jamestown colony put it, "Trust is the mother of deceit."

One story from Grenville's 1585 expedition illustrates this theory of human relations. The company was well entertained with bullfights and banquets by the Spanish colonists on Puerto Rico when Grenville stopped there on the way to Roanoke. The journal went on to say that the Spaniards had been hospitable only because of the large and vigilant English forces. "If they had been stronger than we," it argued, the English would have suffered at their hands. To allow oneself to be vulnerable was to invite contempt, which the English could not allow. People of this period seem to have felt that those who were vulnerable were responsible for whatever happened to them; blame attached to them as much as to anyone who attacked or cheated them. Conversely, when one was vulnerable, the assumption was that someone would inevitably take advantage of that fact. Therefore, the colonists in Roanoke not only came with experience of a situation in which revenge and reprisal were fixtures, but also with the theoretical underpinnings to make sense of that experience.

Even those who argued most strongly for a peaceful approach in America went on to say that force must follow if the Indians proved recalcitrant. The elder Hakluyt recommended sending experienced soldiers, partly for defense against the Spanish if they should attack, but also against the Indians. The Reverend Richard Hakluyt and Hariot said the Indians were poorly armed and relatively weak and therefore could be overawed with English weapons. In 1587 Hakluyt said a hundred men could accomplish in America what it had taken an army of a thousand to do in Ireland. This was the fatal flaw in planning for the Lane colony: because of the common obsession with never showing vulnerability, the pacific approach was not given a real chance however strongly it was believed in. Whether the Indians would have allowed a substantial number of English people peacefully to share their environment will never be known.

Early experience looked hopeful. The Amadas-Barlowe reconnaissance mission of 1584 enjoyed good relations with the Carolina Algonquians. The day after the lone Indian came aboard their ships and then returned their hospitality with fish, a large group of Indians came to them. This was the beginning of an important friendship because the group included Granganimeo, identified to them as the king's brother, who had been placed on the island, according to Carolina Algonquian custom, to oversee that part of the Roanoke domain. The English were struck by the civil and mannerly behavior of these Indians as well as their handsome appearance. When they were opposite the ships, Granganimeo's attendants spread a long mat on the ground; he sat at one end and four chief men sat at the other. The rest of the party stood some distance off. When the English came to them, fully armed, they were surprised to see that the Indians showed no fear; rather, Granganimeo beckoned to them to come and sit by him. He then performed a ceremony of welcome, accompanied, as Barlowe said, by "all signs of joy." He struck his head and his breast and then did the like to the English, which they interpreted as meaning that they were "all one." He made a long speech, which none of the English understood, and then the explorers gave him "divers things," for which he was grateful.

Barlowe was interested in the extreme respect the Indians showed for their leader; none of them dared to speak during the entire ceremony, except the four seated at the other end of the mat who "spake one in the other's ear very softly." When the English distributed some gifts among those four, Granganimeo rose and took the things from them and put them in his own basket. He told the expedition's leaders in sign language that these and all the others were just his servants and followers and that all distribution was to be through him. They later understood that the king himself, whose name was Wingina, had not come because he had been badly wounded in a battle. The 1584 explorers did not see him, though he was important in the story of the Lane colony.

Within the next few days, the expedition began serious trading with the Roanoke Indians, the tribe of Wingina and Granganimeo. The Indians brought deer skins and, so Barlowe claimed, buffalo hides. Granganimeo was taken with a bright tin dish, which he pierced and hung around his neck by a thong. The English thought he was imitating their armor, but we know important men wore such gorgets made of copper. In addition to tin dishes, the Indians most prized knives, axes, and hatchets; they especially wanted metal swords to replace their wooden ones, but trade in swords was forbidden.

Barlowe's description allows us to know a good deal about the previous history of the Outer Banks. It is clear that these Indians were already experienced in trade with Europeans. They knew precisely what the English wanted. They also knew what among the various offerings of the expedition was most useful. They were shrewd consumers, not satisfied with "toys and baubles," but demanding products that would make their traditional life easier and more efficient. They had no metal tools, nor did they have the technology for smelting; the copper they used was soft enough to hammer into shape. Knives, hatchets, and axes clearly made them more effective in their own tasks; swords would have given them superiority over their enemies. Despite English hopes, they were not ready to abandon their own lifestyles and take up European. They wanted to enhance their own lives with European goods, just as the English hoped to do with American products.

Some days later Granganimeo again came to the English; this time he came aboard their ships and drank their wine and ate their bread and meat, which he "liked exceedingly." The Indians had no fermented beverages, so the wine must have been very strange to him. In another few days, he brought his wife, whom Barlowe described as short, "very well favored," and "very bashful," and several small children. She and her women wore bracelets and earrings of copper and pearls as large as peas, which interested the English very much. Barlowe said the Indians were all "yellowish" in color, with black hair, but that the children's hair was sometimes auburn or chestnut. Once Granganimeo had brought his family to them, people of all sorts came forward to trade with the English; they brought skins, something, probably of bone or shell, that Barlowe thought was coral, and various dyes. Trading was general except when Granganimeo was present; then only he and others wearing insignia of high rank traded.

As these contacts went on, Barlowe became increasingly impressed with the respect Indians had for their leaders. Granganimeo's wife moved in great state, accompanied always by a large number of women. The werowance himself always came with a following; as he approached the English, he would build one fire on the shore afar off for every boat accompanying him, so the English would know in advance the size of his party. He very much wanted English armor and a sword and offered a large box of pearls for them. The expedition's leaders refused because they did not want the Indians to know how much Europeans valued pearls until they knew their source.[2]

One of Granganimeo's noble qualities was always keeping his word. Sometimes the English gave him their trading goods without immediately receiving what they had been promised, but they always got what they were owed within the day. He sent them gifts constantly, sometimes a brace or two of fat bucks, hares, or fish: "the best of the world." He also offered them various fruits, nuts, and vegetables, and introduced them to Indian corn. Barlowe thought the land was exceptionally fruitful and was impressed with the promise of Indian agriculture.

Barlowe took seven men and explored the Outer Banks from their base on Hatarask Island. They visited Granganimeo's palisaded village on the northern end of Roanoke Island, near where the colony would eventually be settled. The king's brother was not at home, but his wife came running to greet them. She had her people draw the English boats well up on shore to avoid the currents and "appointed" others to carry the men on their backs up to dry ground and to bring up their oars, which she thought might otherwise be stolen. Her house was, according to Barlowe, divided into rooms. The explorers' clothes were washed and dried, and some of the women washed their stockings and then their feet in warm water.

Meanwhile, their hostess was overseeing everything, including preparation of a "solemn banquet" for them. They were offered corn cooked in broth, venison and fish, both roasted and stewed, and all kinds of roots and fruits. The visitors were served water in which various herbs, including, they thought, cinnamon, ginger, and sassafras, had been steeped. Barlowe was entranced by this reception and thought the food delicious.

> We were entertained with all love, and kindness, and with as much bounty, after their manner, as they could possibly devise. We found the people most gentle, loving, and faithful, void of all guile, and treason, and such as lived after the manner of the golden age.

In this mood he compared the land to the biblical paradise.

Despite this experience, Barlowe was true to his culture's view of human relations; he never really trusted his hostess. While they were eating, several men returned from hunting carrying their bows and arrows; the explorers immediately began to reach for their weapons. As soon as she saw this, Granganimeo's wife sent men out to take the weapons away from those who were approaching; their bows and arrows were broken and the men sent away again. Still the English refused her invitation to spend the night there, which made her "very sorry." She gave them pots containing food for their supper. When they had anchored their boats some way off, she instructed men and women to sit on the bank nearest them all night and sent "fine mats" to the boats to shelter the explorers from the rain. She continued to implore them to spend the night in her village, and was "much grieved" that they would not. Barlowe commented that they could not because the expedition was so small that to risk these men might mean failure for all, even though he reiterated that he had found the people to be the most "kind and loving" in the world.

Those to whom Barlowe reported could justifiably believe that all the ingredients were present for a good and profitable relationship with the Carolina Algonquians. He presented the Indians as friendly and in awe of the English, as well as eager and knowledgeable traders. Manteo and Wanchese, the two Indians Barlowe and Amadas brought back to England, made a great impression on most of those who saw them; their growing command of English made them a tremendous asset in future good relations, though a German visitor to England thought they "made a most childish and silly figure."

One warlike episode may have been omitted. The expedition's two ships apparently parted as they left Roanoke; Barlowe went directly home to England, and Amadas and Fernandes in the flagship went north to Chesapeake Bay where they apparently encountered Indian hostility. An English castaway from the Lane expedition, interrogated by the Spanish in Jamaica, told a garbled version of the 1584 voyage in which he said the English made one landing where they were confronted by "wild" Indians who ate thirty-eight Englishmen. This account may have been a wildly exaggerated version of an actual conflict.

The men of the second expedition, the great fleet that converged on Roanoke in 1585, came expecting cooperation from the Carolina Algonquians; but because of the accident to the *Tiger* and the loss of the colonists' supplies, they were also extremely dependent on Indian aid. When these factors combined with the characteristic expectation of treachery, they made a volatile mix. Someone on the *Tiger,* possibly John White, kept a journal whose entries are normally very terse; for example, under June, "The 26. we came to anchor at Wococon." A similar short entry records their sending word from Wococon to Wingina to tell him of their arrival. On the 11th of July, Grenville set out with a large company in several boats to explore the mainland. One-line entries record their stopping at various Indian towns, in only one case adding any information: at Secoton, the chief village of the Secotan tribe, the explorers "were well entertained there of the Savages."

The next day, they discovered that a silver cup was missing from their baggage. Grenville sent a boat under Amadas' command to retrieve it from the village of Aquascogoc, which they had previously visited. The terse style records in a single sentence the way in which the English philosophy of human relations destroyed all possible hope of peaceful and trusting friendship: "not receiving it according to his promise, we burnt, and spoiled their corn, and Town, all the people being fled." The English feared that to have allowed the theft, if it actually occurred, to go unpunished was to open the door to all kinds of threats to their safety, because it would make them seem weak. They could see no alternative to massive reprisals for the slightest infraction. In fact, though Grenville was shortly to return to England, those who remained were weak indeed and had to depend on the Indians around them for survival.

By this time, the English had achieved a fairly clear picture of relationships among the Indians on whom they were intruding, though we will never be able to determine with complete certainty the tribes and their jurisdictions and relationships from colonists' accounts. Wingina was chief of the Roanoke tribe, which included Wanchese, who accompanied Amadas and Barlowe to England. The tribe's principal seat was on the mainland opposite the island at Dasemunkepeuc. One of White's portraits is thought to be of a woman from Dasemunkepeuc. He did many paintings in Pomeiooc, which may also have been a Roanoke village; he painted the palisaded village as well as several of its inhabitants.

Tribal territory included Roanoke Island, where Granganimeo, Wingina's brother, oversaw a settlement. He came to the Grenville fleet while it was at Wococon and apparently invited the English to settle near his tribe on Roanoke Island. The European goods that flowed into the Roanoke tribe through their association with the colonists enhanced the status and power of Wingina and his people in relations with other Indians. Since Roanoke, like all the Outer Banks, is relatively infertile, it is doubtful that this was a permanent village site, which may explain the tribe's willingness to have the English settle there.

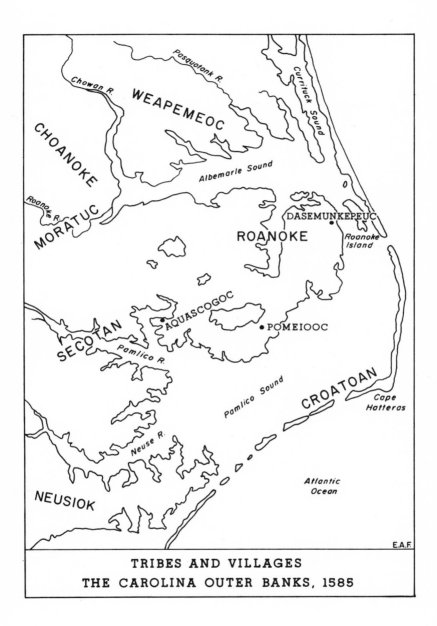

Chowan R.

Pasquotank R.

Currituck Sound

WEAPEMEOC

CHOANOKE

Roanoke R.

MORATUC

Albemarle Sound

DASEMUNKEPEUC

ROANOKE

Roanoke Island

AQUASCOGOC

POMEIOOC

SECOTAN

Pamlico R.

Pamlico Sound

CROATOAN

Cape Hatteras

Neuse R.

Atlantic Ocean

NEUSIOK

E.A.F.

TRIBES AND VILLAGES
THE CAROLINA OUTER BANKS, 1585

The island of Wococon, on which the Grenville fleet first landed, was uninhabited. Both it and Croatoan, directly north of it, were part of the Outer Banks proper. Wococon does not exist today; it is divided between Portsmouth and Ocracoke islands. Croatoan has also changed its form; in the sixteenth century it was a considerable center, a place where great council meetings of several tribes were held. The Croatoan tribe, which maintained the longest friendly relationship with the colonists, were later called the Hatteras Indians. Manteo, the other Indian who went to England in 1584, was a Croatoan.

Grenville explored the area west of Wococon, along the Pamlico River. This entire region was under the control of the Secotan tribe, later called the Machapunga Indians. John White was clearly with Grenville, and many of his paintings are of these Indians and their villages. Aquascogoc was a settlement of the Secotan tribe, whose chief town was called Secoton by the English. On this exploration, they also called at Pomeiooc, which was inhabited by either Secotan or Roanoke Indians.

Ralph Lane was later to explore the region west of Roanoke and to expand English understanding of the political realities they faced. Lane's expedition took him into the territory of the Choanoke Indians, who controlled the area west of Albemarle Sound. The Choanokes were the strongest and most numerous tribe in the area; their king, Menatonon, was said to be chief of eighteen towns and as many as twenty-five thousand people. Lane described Menatonon as a man of great understanding and reputation, though he was apparently crippled. He could field a substantial force, and the governor thought he had other tribes under him. Lane said he learned more from Menatonon about the entire country than he had learned from all his other exploration and discussion.

On this expedition Lane also met the Moratuc Indians along the modern Roanoke River and the Weapemeocs, who were north of Albemarle Sound. The Weapemeocs, whose chief was Okisko, were said to be under the control of Menatonon. Both the Weapemeocs and Menatonon's Choanokes were intermittently allied with Wingina and the Roanokes. What the colonists saw as formal alliance or overlordship probably resulted from chiefs calling on their kin in other tribes for assistance and support.

We know almost nothing of life in Lane's colony over the winter. He sent one party north to the area of Chesapeake Bay to explore in hopes of finding a deepwater bay and a good location for a permanent colony. They probably left in the fall and returned in late winter. Hariot or White, or both, may have been along. White's map of the region shows that someone had done exacting survey work on parts of Chesapeake Bay. Hariot said the travelers slept in the open air on the ground. Lane says almost nothing about what they did except that they received parties of Indians from various tribes and established an English interest there. It is likely that he was being deliberately vague in order to foil Spanish, or even other English, attempts to find the places described.

For the main party of colonists, the story picks up again in the spring. In March, Lane began his exploration to the west of Albemarle Sound. Though Wingina and his people were described as initially delighted at having the English so close, relations had deteriorated by that time. Since we have only Lane's account of the troubles, together with some hints by Hariot about the cruelty of the governor's policy, it takes a good deal of reading between the lines to piece out what had happened. It is difficult because Lane's account is extremely confusing, probably deliberately so.

The first blow was the death of Granganimeo, which must have happened sometime in late winter or early spring. When he died, Wingina announced that his name was now Pemisapan. It is not clear why Wingina changed his name at the death of his brother; Pemisapan may have been a war name he assumed in preparation for driving the English away or it may have been emblematic of his grief. The name implied a watchful, wary attitude in the Algonquian language. With Granganimeo gone, the colonists had lost a powerful voice in Wingina's council, but the main reason why Pemisapan/Wingina turned against them from this point forward probably lay in Lane's arrogance, which we can only guess at, and especially in the pressure that the colonists' demands for food placed on native reserves. Though it is clear that the Carolina Algonquians' agriculture produced a surplus, it is unlikely that they were prepared to keep over a hundred extra people alive until the next harvest. Hariot's account says the colony lived on native food for all but twenty days, which gives an idea of the magnitude of the problem they presented the Roanokes.

After Granganimeo's death, his brother moved the tribal capital temporarily to the island, probably to watch the settlers' activities

more closely. The Roanoke colonists were not immediately aware that
Pemisapan/Wingina had decided on war against them. Lane consulted
him about his idea of exploring on the mainland, and the chief strongly
urged him to go. He said that Menatonon, chief of the Choanokes, was
holding a great council of all his allies with as many as three thousand
bowmen in attendance, to discuss what to do about the colony. Lane
later found out that Pemisapan/Wingina had sent ahead to tell Menatonon the English were coming. Despite his swaggering attitude, Lane
could not conceal the almost total dependence of the colonists on the
Indians. If vulnerability invited treachery, as they thought, then they
were natural victims. Lane explained that he was forced to divulge his
plans to Pemisapan/Wingina because he could not have moved without
guides from the Roanokes. Thus, he left himself open to the double
cross in which Pemisapan/Wingina informed the Indians to the west of
Lane's plans.

Nonetheless, Lane said he burst in on the meeting led by Menatonon
and caught them unawares, thus gaining the upper hand. He captured
Menatonon and held him for two days until the chief offered an accept-
able ransom. Menatonon's son, Skiko, was kept a prisoner and was sent
to Roanoke to ensure his father's cooperation. It was during his own
two days' captivity that Menatonon told Lane about all the Indians on
the mainland and the resources that might interest the English. Lane
was impressed with Menatonon's gravity and wisdom, and Menatonon
apparently decided to cooperate with the English, or at least to let
them think he was compliant. He told Lane that the great meeting
against the colonists had been "wholly procured by Pemisapan himself." Menatonon offered not only information but guides and other
aid for any exploration Lane wanted to attempt.

Of all the sites and peoples described, two piqued Lane's attention.
Menatonon outlined a journey to the northeast that would take the
colonists to a stronghold on a deepwater bay—just the kind of place
Lane was looking for. It is probable that he was describing a part of
Chesapeake Bay, but it was not clear to Lane that it was the same area
his party had visited earlier. Menatonon made the land sound very
attractive to English ears. From the Choanokes' point of view, it would
be a good location for the newcomers: far enough away to free the
Carolina Indians from English demands for food and other assistance,
but close enough to obtain trade goods.

Menatonon said the "king" of that province found so many pearls in the bay that he and his principal followers covered their clothing, beds, and houses with them. Clearly the colonists had been less than successful in concealing their interest in pearls. That same king had visited Menatonon two years before and had offered to sell him pearls, he said, but at too high a price in copper. Menatonon did show Lane a string of pearls, but they were misshapen and black, though some were of great size, and a few "very orient and round." He assured the governor that the king to the northeast had beautiful white pearls that were obtained from deep water; these black ones were only from the shallow. Lane wondered whether those Indians had an established trade with some Europeans for whom the white pearls were reserved. Menatonon warned Lane against venturing northeastward with too small a party; that king, he said, was very strong with a skilled and courageous army, and he would resist the entrance of any strangers into his country, especially if they intended to "meddle with the fishing for any Pearl there." Despite the warning, though, he offered guides if Lane wished to make the attempt.

In his report Lane generated an elaborate scheme for traveling to that territory, which he had intended to put into practice as soon as Grenville arrived with sufficient supplies, ships, and men. The great detail and elaborateness of the plan may be Lane's attempt to forestall criticism of his failure to carry out the exploration. He was trying to show the seriousness of his intentions. His plans involved dividing the expedition in half, with one party going in a bark and two pinnaces by sea from Roanoke to Chesapeake Bay. The other, two hundred strong, would have taken all the small boats and, with Menatonon's guides, have gone up the Choanoke River and then overland.

Lane would have ensured Menatonon's cooperation in giving him loyal and experienced guides by having Skiko, "his best beloved son," handcuffed to him the entire time. As the men marched overland, Lane would have had them build a small fort, or sconce, every two days' march to cover their retreat. Twenty-five or thirty men would have been left in a palisaded enclosure to guard the boats, and then fifteen or twenty others would have stayed behind in each fort. Ideally each sconce should be built next to an Indian cornfield to afford the men a food supply. Had the site on Chesapeake Bay turned out to be as described and "worth the possession," he would have erected a major fort and eventually moved the entire colony there.

The idea of erecting a fort every two days' march was taken directly from Lane's Irish experience; it was a common strategy there. He explained that his men would never be in danger of being cut off and that the river current would swiftly carry them back to Albemarle Sound if they were threatened. Lane's plans make very clear his intention of moving against any and all Indians in a military manner, and his expectation that violence would be a normal part of all such meetings. He had moved very far from the instructions with which he arrived.

Since he did not yet feel ready to undertake the expedition to Chesapeake Bay, Lane decided to act on the other possibility he had gleaned from what Menatonon told him. Far to the west, there was supposed to be a place called Chaunis Temoaton which had some kind of rich mines. The "marvelous mineral" from there was called *wassador* by the Indians, he said, but he added that they called all metals *wassador*. He was told that it was the color of English copper, but pale and soft. Skiko described the western Indians' method of panning for copper ore in a swift-moving stream issuing out of the mountains, using a large bowl partially covered by a skin. The ore was melted over a fire and yielded two parts of metal for five parts of ore. Lane apparently thought the ore might be gold, or at the least very high-quality copper. Skiko said it was highly esteemed in that country, and the people had great plates made of it. He had not been there himself; it was twenty days' journey farther west than he had ever been.

The idea of locating a mine, especially if there were a chance it might be a gold mine, was especially attractive to the colonists. Lane found willing volunteers for this expedition because all the soldiers hoped to benefit personally from such a find. There were also some hints that the river on which they traveled issued from near a saltwater source; they might find the passage to the South Sea at the same time they found the mine. Lane set out with two boats and forty men, with some supplies but expecting to be fed by the Indians along the way; he thought that he had made an agreement with the Moratuc Indians to that effect when he had surprised them at Menatonon's council. What he found was quite different.

Pemisapan/Wingina had "sent word" to Indians along Lane's route telling them that he was coming and that he intended to kill them. They all withdrew away from the river, carrying their corn with them; in three days' journey, Lane reported, they saw not one person, nor could they find a grain of corn in the Indian towns they passed. Lane protested in his account that they had "no intention to be hurtful to any of them," but also acknowledged that his was a warlike expedition. The governor addressed his company, telling them that they were one hundred sixty miles from home with only two days' supplies and without hope of any more. It was his conviction that Pemisapan/Wingina had urged him to go on the venture in the hope that he and his party would die on the way, which Lane referred to with his customary arrogance as the "treason of our own Savages."

Lane put the case as accurately as he could and asked his men to spend the night deliberating whether they would rather adventure their last two days' supplies in further exploration or return home now safely. To his delight the soldiers next morning told him that they would go on as long as they had one pint of corn per man left. They pointed to the two mastiff dogs accompanying them, adding that they would make a good stew with sassafras leaves if the situation became critical. Eating the mastiffs would supply them for two days during which they could float on the current back down to the sound, where they could take fish from Indian weirs. Lane acted as devil's advocate, arguing the opposite opinion, but he was proud of his men's resolution. The fact that they hoped to find a mine was apparently a powerful incentive. Lane even thought they could turn the unexpected hostility of the Indians to their benefit, because if there were a clash he could capture some and force them to be his guides.

When open conflict occurred shortly thereafter, Lane was careful to point out that it was begun by the Indians. As he described it, some Indians called out to Manteo, who was in Lane's boat, about three in the afternoon and then began to sing. Lane hoped that it was a song of welcome, but Manteo quickly disabused him; they meant to fight. The Indians let fly a volley of arrows, injuring none of the English, and were answered by fire from the boats. By the time the explorers had landed, the Indians were gone, fled into the woods. Lane realized that even if he pursued them the next day and found them, a most unlikely possibility, no food would be forthcoming; so he decided to set out for home base the next morning before dawn. The Indian attack had achieved its goal. This time his men were ready to agree, "for they were now come to their dogs porridge, that they had bespoken for themselves."

The return journey downriver, a four-day trip against the current, took only one day. The men were by this time reduced to eating sassafras leaves alone. They were unable to cross the sound because of high winds and so were entirely without food that day, Easter eve. Easter morning, April 3rd, was calm, so they crossed the sound and raided the weirs of a Weapemeoc village, from which all the inhabitants had fled. On Monday morning they arrived back at Roanoke. Lane told this story of their hardships in such great detail because he wanted to convince the backers in England that he had truly tried as hard as was humanly possible to accomplish two of the company's aims: locating a mine and a passage to the South Sea. The story of this expedition became famous. Captain John Smith, in the later Jamestown colony, once shamed his reluctant and fearful men by recounting the story of the bravery and sacrifice of Lane's party.

The colonists thought they had been promised that Grenville would be back from England with new settlers and supplies by Easter, so Lane and his men believed they would not have to live long with the consequences of their actions. It must have been a time of anxious waiting for them. In fact, Grenville and his fleet were still in England, so help from that source was a long way off. Grenville and Raleigh were mindful of the colony's plight, but 1585–1586 was a busy year for Raleigh: he had been given important new offices in the West of England and was occupied with plans for the colonization of his plantations in Munster. Grenville devoted much of the winter to gathering supplies and preparing ships to sail in the spring. Late beginnings seem to have been a motif of his life, however; and it was mid-April before the fleet set out. Raleigh had sent a small boat loaded with immediate necessities ahead of the main fleet, but even this had not sailed until after Easter. Mixed with Lane's defensiveness when he told his story was a pronounced note of complaint that the settlers had never had the support they expected, partly because of accidents, but also because of such delays.

During the month of April the English became acutely aware of the extent of their dependence on Indian aid, a situation Lane made no attempt to hide in his account. Pemisapan/Wingina had decided, he said, to take his people and leave the island without planting any crops. Had he done so, Lane reported, the English would necessarily have starved. "For at that time we had no weirs for fish, neither could our men skill of the making of them, neither had we one grain of corn for seed to put into the ground." However superior they thought their technology to be, they were helpless in that environment. He reported that the Indians' perception of the colonists had also undergone a dramatic change. While he was gone, rumors had been spread that he and his party were dead or starving. Those Indians who had formerly been receptive to Hariot's preaching of Christianity now began to question and even, according to Lane, to blaspheme "and flatly to say, that our Lord God was not God, since he suffered us to sustain much hunger" and even to be killed by other Indians.

When Lane and his party returned, much of the murmuring stopped; Pemisapan/Wingina was startled to see that he and all his men had survived. Further, Lane said, when Manteo and the other Indians who had accompanied him reported that for the most part the mighty tribes among whom the expedition had traveled had not directly challenged them, and reminded their listeners that Lane had captured Menatonon and still held Skiko prisoner, the Roanokes began to reconsider. Though Granganimeo was dead, there was still one voice in the council urging caution in dealing with the English. This man was Ensenore, whom Lane described as a "savage father" to Pemisapan. Ensenore believed that the English were servants of a powerful god and that they were not subject to injury by the Indians because, as Hariot described, the colonists were dead men risen from the grave who had the power to kill at a distance. He feared that resistance to the English would result in the destruction of the Roanokes. Pemisapan, according to Lane, began again to believe in the special powers of the colonists when they returned from the venture on which he had sent them to their deaths.

Pemisapan/Wingina's caution about challenging Lane directly was increased a few days later when a messenger arrived from Menatonon. He carried pearls, which Lane thought were meant as a present; when Pemisapan told him they were sent as a ransom for Skiko, Lane refused them. The more important mission of this embassy was to inform Lane that Menatonon had "commanded" Okisko, chief of the Weapemeocs, "to yield himself servant, and homager, to the great Werowanza of England, and after her to Sir Walter Raleigh." From this time forward, Queen Elizabeth was to be the sole sovereign of the Weapemeocs. Significantly, twenty-four men were sent to Pemisapan by Okisko to inform him of this submission. The idea that Menatonon could command action on the part of another tribe derives from the English propensity to interpret Indian affairs in terms of familiar European models. Okisko may have been related to Menatonon and may have been responding to a call on his kinship obligations. When the time for action actually came, Okisko withdrew into the interior, and the tribe split over whether to join Wingina against the English. Neither Menatonon nor Okisko could literally command the Weapemeocs to act in a certain way.

Menatonon's call for the Weapemeocs to cooperate with the English left the Roanokes dangerously exposed for the moment. Clearly there was considerable maneuvering by the Indians, to whom the English were both a threat and a potential help, to establish the most advantageous relationship. Menatonon, situated farther away, could court the colonists without incurring the risk of their imposing on his people as they had on the Roanokes. A strong bond with the Europeans would enhance his power over the other tribes in the region if he became the distributor of trade goods and the main intermediary between the two cultures. He was also concerned to protect his son Skiko, still a prisoner in the colony.

Pemisapan/Wingina's behavior to the English changed dramatically; he helped them in the most fundamental way he could. His men came and built fish weirs for the colony and sowed large fields with crops for them; he also gave the English plots in which they could sow their own seeds. Since the Roanokes had already been reported as ready to abandon these fields in favor of their more fertile mainland plots, this may have been less of a concession than Lane thought. Lane was optimistic now; he thought the promised harvest would have been sufficient for the entire company for a year. The colony now had only two difficult months to get through; harvest would take place in early July.

Then suddenly another disaster struck; Ensenore died on April 20th, "the only friend to our nation that we had amongst them." Now there was no one to speak for the English in Roanoke councils, and many came forward to urge aggressive action. Lane must have been stunned to learn that Wanchese, one of the Indians who had been in England and on whom the colony relied, was strongly urging Pemisapan/Wingina to move against the settlement. The first step in the Roanokes' plan was to weaken the English by denying them provisions. A general agreement was made that no one would sell the colonists food. The Roanokes came in the night, removed the fish from the weirs they had made for the settlers, and then broke the weirs, knowing that the English were helpless to repair them.

This strategy had its desired effect; Lane was forced to break his company up into small bands and send them out to live off the country as best they could. Captain Edward Stafford was sent to Croatoan Island and his group of twenty had the additional task of looking out for any sign of European ships. Another smaller group went to Hatarask, and several parties were sent to the mainland opposite Roanoke Island. Lane said they lived on oysters and cassava, by which he apparently meant a member of the arum family, probably golden-club, which grows in swampy areas.

Pemisapan, who had moved his base to the mainland, naturally thought it would be an easy matter to deal with the colonists, dispersed as they were. The governor thought that he had left the island to get away from the colonists' constant demands for food, which Lane said were met with excuses because Pemisapan did not have the courage to reject them out of hand. Lane, with his limited sense of reality, did not stop to consider that the burden of feeding his large company over the winter must have made the Roanokes' supplies short indeed, and that it was not only policy, but also reality, that made Pemisapan deny them further food. There is some indication that the Indians, like the colonists, were living off the land until the harvest came in.

Pemisapan's plan, as Lane described it, was massive. The Roanokes held a large council meeting to commemorate Ensenore and console themselves for the loss of their great leader. Okisko and the Weapomeocs were invited despite their newly proclaimed allegiance to Queen Elizabeth and were offered "great quantity of copper" to partici-pate in the planned attack. Lane's account of Pemisapan's maneuver-ing allows greater insight into the enduring realities of Carolina Algon-quian relationships than does his own ethnocentric interpretation based on European models. The Roanokes did not perceive the Weapomeocs as forever committed to alliance with the English or bound by Menatonon's command. When the issue came to a trial, Okisko and his tribe followed the traditional noncoercive path.

The story of the Roanoke chief's attempts to assemble a large army, though, also demonstrates how the coming of the English had changed local relationships. The Roanokes, as the principal recipients of English trade goods, paid in return for the corn they were forced to sell the settlers, could now offer substantial inducements to other tribes to support them, inducements of a magnitude that would not have been available before. The balance in the region was drastically changed by the influx of the new and desirable commodities the Europeans had to offer. The scope of political activity may have been altered also. Lane claimed that forces were solicited even from as far away as Chesapeake Bay.

The plan was for Pemisapan/Wingina to execute Lane and his principal officers, and then by fires to signal a general attack that would dispatch the rest of the colonists. Tarraquine and Andacon, whom Lane identified as important men in Pemisapan's following and "very lusty fellows," were to accomplish the initial attack with about twenty men. They planned to set fire to the thatched roof of Lane's cabin in the middle of the night; then, as he ran from his house in his shirt, "they would have knocked out my brains." A similar fate was planned for Hariot and "all the rest of our better sort," with all the individual houses being set on fire at the same time. The plan included an attack on the fort as well as the houses outside it.

Okisko, chief of the Weapemeocs, sent word that he and his principal men would not participate; in fact they and their immediate tribesmen were moving farther into the mainland. The effect of this, apparently, was to free other Weapemeocs to take part if they wished. Lane reported that one other tribe, the Mandoags, who were probably Iroquoian, definitely agreed to participate. Pemisapan offered all who came in "great impress of copper in hand," along with "large promises" of spoils to come. Warriors may have planned to join as individuals, as in the Weapomeoc case, rather than in tribal units.

The assembly was to take place on June 10, but Lane had advance warning from Skiko, his prisoner. Lane, who prided himself on his iron discipline, had put Skiko in leg irons after an escape attempt, and had threatened execution until Pemisapan had made him see the folly of that. Pemisapan assumed that Skiko must hate the English as he now did and befriended the prisoner when he was again allowed some freedom on the island. Skiko visited Pemisapan and, as they dined, learned all about the conspiracy. The boy had apparently come to like his English captors; Lane said that he was "well used at my hand" and the soldiers "made much of him." He was also aware that his father, Menatonon, wanted to keep the relationship friendly for reasons of his own. Therefore, Skiko revealed Pemisapan's plans to Lane.

Lane now developed a counter strategy. He first determined to put Pemisapan/Wingina off his guard by sending word that he had decided to go to Croatoan Island because he had heard of the arrival of the English fleet, "(though I in truth had neither heard nor hoped for so good adventure)." The messenger was to say that Lane would come to Pemisapan to "borrow" men to hunt and fish for him on Croatoan and also to buy four days' supply of corn. Pemisapan replied that he would come to Roanoke instead, but he kept making excuses and putting off the day. Lane thought he was waiting for his allies, who were to begin arriving in about a week. On May 31, Pemisapan hastily assembled all the Indians he could for a meeting on Roanoke Island, though he was still at Dasemunkepeuc on the mainland opposite. Lane decided to go to Pemisapan with a large company, but to attack the Indians gathered on Roanoke beforehand in what he called a "camisado," a night assault in which the attackers kept their shirttails out in back so they would not be shot accidentally by their compatriots. Lane's surprise attack was forestalled. He sent soldiers to gather up the Indians' canoes at sunset so that no one could inform Pemisapan on the mainland of what was happening. The party surprised a canoe with two Indians in it, whom they killed, but with a good deal of noise, which revealed the warlike plans of the English. In fact, Lane said, the Indians encamped on the island had become as wary as he and were closely following all the English actions, so genuine surprise would not have been possible.

Now that the alarm was raised, both sides began to fire, and three or four Indians were killed; the rest fled into the woods. Next morning Lane took twenty-five men and his highest-ranking officers to the mainland to confront Pemisapan. They sent an Indian who met them at the shore to tell the chief that they were going to Croatoan and had come to him on the way to complain of Osocon, one of his principal men, who had attempted to remove Skiko from Roanoke. Skiko was described as being back in chains, though this may have been a ruse to enhance the idea that he was not friendly to the English.

Pemisapan admitted Lane into his presence; he was surrounded by seven or eight of his council. Lane then gave the agreed signal, shouting "Christ our victory," and the attack began. Pemisapan was shot and thought dead, and the others were quickly accounted for. Lane was busy protecting some Indians whom he identified as Manteo's friends, possibly Croatoan Indians temporarily with Pemisapan. Suddenly Pemisapan jumped up and ran away as if he had not been touched by a bullet; he outran the company, except that "mine Irish boy" shot him "thwart the buttocks" with Lane's petronell, a heavy pistol carried in the belt. Another Irish servant of Lane's, Edward Nugent, and the unnamed deputy provost followed Pemisapan into the woods. Lane despaired of capturing him and feared for the two men's lives, when he spotted Nugent emerging from the woods "with Pemisapan's head in his hand."

Lane never mentioned Indian relations again in his narrative, and in fact the colony did not remain much longer in America. The effects of Lane's policy would be reaped by the next group of settlers, those who came under John White in 1587. We know that not everyone believed in Lane's conspiracy theory. Thomas Hariot's report of the colony said openly that "some of our company towards the end of the year, showed themselves too fierce, in slaying some of the people, in some towns, upon causes that on our part, might easily enough have been borne withall." We will never know how much of Lane's policy was a self-fulfilling prophecy that caused to happen those things he expected or feared.

Pemisapan was killed on June 1, 1586. A week later Lane received the news he was waiting for: Captain Stafford on Croatoan Island had sighted a "great Fleet of 23 sails," though it was not yet known whether they were friend or foe.

6

THE DEBATE OVER COLONIES

The Roanoke colonists were lucky; the great fleet was that of Sir Francis Drake, who had been away from England almost as long as they had. Drake's commission to strike at the Spanish empire had been the key English strategy in opening the sea war with Spain in 1585. For almost a year he had been terrorizing Spanish settlements, a campaign capped by his looting of Santo Domingo and Cartagena. He was so effective that he forced colonial authorities to begin planning for reorganization of the empire's defences and the system by which treasure was sent to Spain. The threat of future exploits by Drake and others may also have led Philip II of Spain to decide to strike directly at England, the source of his problem, with the Great Armada of 1588.

Sir Francis Drake's decision to call at Roanoke was probably made before his or Grenville's fleet ever left England. He expected to be the first of many privateers who would use the base to be established there. Had the Outer Banks offered a suitable harbor, and had Grenville's company stayed over the winter as expected, then the arrival of Drake's fleet would have been a fair test of the colony's usefulness. As it was, Lane and his colonists had little to offer Drake. He, for his part, had been busy on their behalf according to his own lights. When his men stormed Santo Domingo and Cartagena, Drake rescued a very large number of slaves and Indians from Spanish clutches. The few European galley slaves among them he intended to keep, but he decided to offer the three hundred to five hundred others to the colony, probably as a labor supply.

Drake did the cause of English colonization another service on the way to Roanoke, though its long-range benefit was doubtful. As his fleet passed Florida, he attacked the newly built fort and town of St. Augustine. The fortifications, hastily begun on news of Drake's

approach, were so weak that all the people fled. The English learned
that the town was theirs when a Frenchman who had been a Spanish
prisoner rowed out to the fleet in a little boat playing "the tune of the
Prince of Orange his song" on a small fife, thereby identifying himself
as a Protestant. Drake and his men removed a chest containing treasure to the value of £2,000 sterling with which the Spanish soldiers
were to have been paid, and fourteen "great pieces of Brass Ordnance,"
large guns.

They took advantage of the fact that the colony was built entirely of
timber, burning it completely. As one account put it, "There was
about 250 houses in the Town, but we left not one of them standing."
The only Spaniard they saw was a small child found in a boat newly
come from Spain; they sent the child to the Spanish, but could not get
any of them to come and talk. The cannon were for the Roanoke
colonists, but Drake thought he was doing something more fundamental for their welfare in attacking St. Augustine. The weaker the Spanish colonies near the Outer Banks were, the safer he thought the
English would be. Plans to attack the Spanish settlement at Santa
Elena were scrapped because Drake's fleet lacked a pilot capable of
steering the ships through the dangerous shoals surrounding it.

In early June, the fleet coasted alongside the Outer Banks and spotted Captain Stafford's fire near modern Cape Hatteras. Drake sent a
small boat ashore and picked up a man to guide them to the inlet
opposite Roanoke. The ships were forced to anchor two miles offshore
because of their great draft and the shallowness of the water, ample
illustration of Roanoke's uselessness as a privateering port. The guide
described the colony's situation, so, from his anchorage, Drake wrote
letters offering such help as he could give, a "most bountiful and
honorable offer" according to Lane. He actually gave the governor his
choice between two plans. The first was that Drake would give the
colonists food, clothing, and other necessities, and also completely
manned boats and a small ship suitable for exploring so Lane could
pursue his instructions to look for a deepwater port. Drake assured
Lane that he would leave sufficient supplies and experienced mariners
so that the entire company could be brought home at any time if that
should prove necessary. We can gain some insight into Drake's
method of operation in comparison to Grenville's; he specified that he
had consulted his council before making the offer and that all his chief

men were in agreement. The other choice was simply to go home with Drake's fleet "if they thought they had made sufficient discovery already," certainly a claim Lane was unlikely to make.

Lane asked Drake to include weapons and ammunition in his offer, and to exchange some of his own men for unfit colonists; when he agreed, Lane answered on behalf of his colony that they would stay until the following August and spend the summer exploring. Lane was lavish in his gratitude for this timely help. Drake gave the colonists the bark *Francis*, of seventy tons, freighted it with food for four months, and satisfied all Lane's other requests "to the uttermost." He also gave "two fine pinnaces, and 4 small boats," and, equally important, two of his most experienced masters, Abraham Kendall and Griffith Herne, and "very sufficient" gangs of sailors. All this was concluded on the 12th of June when several of Lane's officers were aboard the *Francis*.

On June 13th, a huge storm blew up, so great that Lane thought it was a miracle the entire fleet was not driven against the shore. He praised Drake's expertise in foreseeing the storm's ferocity and thanked God's protection for saving most of the ships. This "extraordinary and very strange" storm, which lasted three or four days, combined the high winds of a hurricane with thunder and lightning and hail as big as hen's eggs. There were such great waterspouts at sea that one of Drake's men said it looked as if heaven and earth were trying to meet. Several of the boats and small pinnaces were destroyed, and many of the ships broke their anchor cables and were driven out to sea. One of the ships driven away was the *Francis* with some of Lane's officers, old and newly acquired, and the provisions. This must have been reminiscent for Lane and his men of the accident to the *Tiger* and its stores. The colony was plagued from start to finish by these accidents and near misses. We can see how fragile and tenuous the entire colonial enterprise actually was; everything seems to have hung by a thread, which was easily snapped.

In this case, there is more to the story than meets the eye, since the *Francis* could have returned to Roanoke once the storm was over, though it had lost all its anchors. The men on board may have insisted on accompanying Drake's fleet back to England, so that they would be present when the spoils from their many months of privateering were divided. Otherwise, they may have feared complete loss of their shares.

Increasingly the connection with privateering that had been so important in stimulating initial interest in the colony returned to plague every effort at Roanoke and ultimately to doom it to failure. Promoters had hoped that England could have colonies without paying for them; it was only through long and painful lessons that they finally realized this was not possible. The Roanoke colony, from June 1586 on, contributed to that learning process.

After the storm abated, Drake once again consulted his council and came to Lane with another offer. He would dip into his reduced capabilities and give the colonists another ship, the bark *Bonner*, with a good master and pilot. With these Lane could still carry out his plans for exploration until August and then bring his company home, "but he told me that he would not for any thing undertake to have her brought into our harbor." Clearly the bark *Bonner* would be much less suited to coastal exploration than the *Francis* would have been. There was an ominous rider to Drake's second offer; he asked Lane to consult his leading men and then deliver their answer in writing. He may have wanted to make sure that they took full responsibility before Raleigh and his investors in England for whatever decision was made.

Lane said his council was unanimous,

> considering the case that we stood in, the weakness of our company, the small number of the same, the carrying away of our first appointed bark, with those two especial masters, with our principal provisions in the same, by the very hand of God as it seemed, stretched out to take us from thence: considering also that his second offer, though most honorable of his part, yet of ours not to be taken, insomuch as there was no possibility for her with any safety to be brought into the harbor: Seeing furthermore, our hope for supply with Sir Richard Grenville, so undoubtedly promised us before Easter, not yet come, neither then likely to come this year considering the doings in England for Flanders, and also for America, that therefore I would resolve my self, with my company to go into England in that Fleet.

In short the colonists were fed up. Drake agreed to take them, though everyone was going to be cramped in his greatly reduced fleet.

Once the decision to leave was made, the colonists could not get away fast enough. Lane indicated that his haste grew out of consideration for Drake, who had risked his entire fleet and "had in that storm sustained more peril of wrack than in all his former most honorable actions against the Spaniards." The sailors were so concerned about the continuing "boisterous" weather and "much aggrieved with their long and dangerous abode in that miserable road" that they hurried the colonists on board and tossed overboard much of the baggage the settlers tried to bring with them. This was a great loss to us as well as to them; we would know much more about the colony and about early colonization in general if it were not for this incident. Lane said that all their "cards, books, and writings" were thrown away, which may be the reason Thomas Hariot never wrote the full natural history of America that he intended. He lamented the loss of all the specimens collected by him and others as well as of many of his notes.

Lane failed to mention that more than possessions was lost in this hasty departure. A member of Drake's fleet recorded that the colonists abandoned three men who were on a mission into the interior, possibly returning Skiko to his father. These lost colonists were never heard of again. The several hundred freed slaves and Indians collected by Drake for the colony were probably left in Carolina as well, maybe with some of the equipment Drake had taken from St. Augustine. The records are equally silent on their fate, and we have no way of knowing whether they were met by the next group of colonists or not. If they succeeded in melting into the Indian population, then they began a tradition that was to have a long history in that part of America. The Algonquians of North America's east coast apparently lacked the European sense of racial exclusivity; they adopted into their tribes and clans anyone who became culturally one of them, and they did so on terms of equality. It is entirely possible that the people left by Drake lived on and produced descendants who would have been Indians in every sense meaningful to them.

Lane's plea for understanding suggested that the storm that prevented the colonists from accepting Drake's offer meant that "the hand of God" was taking them from America. He could not be expected to stand out against divine providence. Some in England also saw God's will manifested in the colonists' hasty departure, but interpreted it differently. The younger Richard Hakluyt wrote that the colonists left as hurriedly and confusedly

> as if they had been chased from thence by a mighty army, and no doubt
> so they were, for the hand of God came upon them for the cruelty, and
> outrages committed by some of them against the native inhabitants of
> that country.

It was clear that the lessons of the first Roanoke colony remained to be sorted out.

The contents of Hakluyt's next paragraph must have wounded the colonists further; he said the first small supply ship sent by Raleigh arrived immediately after the colonists left "this paradise of the world." Had they held on just a short while longer, the whole venture need not have been scrapped. That ship searched for the colonists for a few days and then returned to England with its supplies. Not only was the arrival of this ship imminent when the colony was deserted, but, according to Hakluyt, Grenville's three ships, "well appointed," were off the Outer Banks two weeks later. Lane and his council must have been filled with a sense of the opportunities lost, though they may have been just as happy to be back in England and away from the situation their presence had created at Roanoke. Grenville was said to have done some exploring, hoping to find news of the settlers; but discovering nothing and finding the settlement "desolate," he also decided there was nothing to do but return to England.

Neither relief expedition mentioned anything about the three men Lane left behind or about the several hundred former captives Drake is thought to have deposited at Roanoke. Since the time elapsed was so short, it seems impossible that they could have completely left the area to live with local Indians. As they did not know the ships' country of origin, they may have judged it wiser simply to keep out of sight during the short time the relief vessels were there, as did the Roanoke Indians. There is one uncorroborated Spanish intelligence report alleging that the first ship found the bodies of an Englishman and an Indian hanged. The fate of all the others is one of the many mysteries surrounding the entire Roanoke enterprise that remain to this day.

Grenville was late in arriving off the Outer Banks, and he may have been much later than Hakluyt indicated; the reason for this, besides his late start, was the old obsession with privateering. Since in the eyes of men like Grenville the colony existed only to aid privateering, there was no reason to let its needs get in the way of the main enterprise. Grenville's fleet spent considerable time in these activities, beginning shortly after leaving England, and he was reckless about the ships he attacked. His first victim was an English ship carrying wines belonging to Breton merchants; the ship was released after its cargo was seized. Next Grenville took two French ships off Cape Finisterre, which he sent back to England, and then a Dutch flyboat, which he made part of his own fleet. His justification for attacking the Dutch ship was that it was trading with the Spanish enemy, supplying food for its squadrons. All this took time and weakened his manpower because each prize ship had to be provided with a crew. Grenville now sailed with little further delay to Roanoke, but the West Indies and the rich prizes to be had there were on his mind.

Grenville probably arrived on the Outer Banks in late July, though it could have been even later. He reported that he made a thorough and determined search for the missing colonists, even exploring areas into which he had not previously ventured. He saw only three Indians, which indicates that they were dealing with his presence by avoiding contact. All three were captured, but two escaped. The third gave Grenville to understand that Drake had removed the entire colony. This man was probably the Indian named Raleigh who later lived in Grenville's household at Bideford. The Bideford parish register carries the following entries:

Anno Domini 1588 Christenings . . .
Raleigh, A Wynganditoian . . . xxvij day of March
Anno Domini 1589 Buryings . . .
Raleigh, A man of Wynganditoia the vijth day of Aprile
sepultus fuit

Grenville, finding nothing and being satisfied that the colonists were gone, now made a gross error of judgment. He still had a large crew, probably three hundred or four hundred men, and all the supplies intended for Lane's colony. He should either have left a large force with all the food and equipment or abandoned the site altogether. Instead, he left a very small holding party of fifteen men, with four "pieces of artillery of cast iron" and supplies for at least a year. Grenville was anxious to be off after the Spanish treasure fleet and may have reasoned from the small number of Indians he saw that there was no danger, though he himself knew how populous the area had been in 1585.

His luck was bad after leaving Roanoke; the treasure ships had left in early August and he found nothing in the West Indies. He arrived in the Azores with a serious outbreak of sickness on his ships, possibly from scurvy. A Spanish pilot whom Grenville had captured to work for him later reported that thirty-four sailors died. Grenville turned the fleet around and sailed to Newfoundland for supplies. He probably hoped to catch the English fishing fleet there and to buy fresh food from them, but he may have been too late. We are told that his men caught fish and rested ashore and then sailed back to the Azores. There he succeeded in capturing two ships, one loaded with hides and the other with sugar and ginger.

These prizes, together with the cargoes picked up on the way out, probably paid for the relief ventures, but did not bring in the spectacular income Grenville had managed on his first Roanoke voyage, and the courts forced him to restore some of what he had taken from French and Dutch ships. Just what had been accomplished by a year's venture at Roanoke remained to be sorted out. Certainly the Spanish had reason to believe they knew what a successful English colony would mean: Hakluyt closed his account of Grenville's voyage by noting that he sailed to the Azores, "on some of which Islands he landed, and spoiled the Towns of all such things as were worth carriage."

What was the future of Roanoke? What lessons could be drawn from experience, and what indications were there that a successful colony could be established? Would such a colony be worth the effort? All these questions had to be answered before any further planning began. The first step was to evaluate the actual results of the first settlement.

The greatest practical achievement of Lane's colony was probably the one he valued least: the fruits of the John White–Thomas Hariot collaboration. Modern people clearly value it most of all, but it was also highly important to intellectuals all over Europe at the time. The seventeenth century witnessed the beginnings of modern science, the Scientific Revolution. It was a time of great excitement for educated men, who believed that all knowledge was coming within their grasp. One of the most attractive aspects of early science was the degree to which it was a group activity; marshaling of information and insights required pooling of knowledge even across national boundaries. The geographical discussions Richard Hakluyt held in France are one example of this kind of sharing.

This quest for all knowledge was, for most, a religious search. Devout scientists believed that human beings had once understood everything about the natural world through God's revelation to Adam. This knowledge had been lost in the intervening centuries through corruption; but it could be recovered, and God progressively revealed new fields to be searched. One of these was America. Most early scientists believed that a vital first step in the recovery of knowledge was to identify and catalogue all the flora and fauna of the earth, so Hariot and White were actually on the frontiers of knowledge as well as on the physical frontier. Their accomplishment was central to the concerns of European intellectuals.

A more immediate positive result of Lane's colony was its demonstration that English people could live in a southern climate. Though promoters had feared that heat alone could kill colonists accustomed to England's moderate temperatures, the venture in fact saw few deaths from disease; Lane attributed this healthiness to the discipline "severely executed" by him in the colony. It was commonly believed that the "meaner sort" of people, left to themselves, would become progressively lazier, and that this moral failing would eventually produce scurvy and other fatal diseases. This belief was reinforced by experience in other colonies, before and after Roanoke, where the lassitude associated with the early phases of lingering diseases was interpreted as laziness. When the more extreme symptoms of diseases such as scurvy became visible, leaders believed it was the laziness, the weak character, of the victim that had brought it on.[1] Roanoke had a remarkably good record of healthfulness; one of the major objections to English settlement in southern areas was therefore overcome.

The colonists had to accomplish more than their own survival, however. The real question was whether there was an economic advantage greater than the costs involved in setting up and sustaining a North American colony. It was the businessmen who would eventually decide whether the venture ended here or continued. One thing was absolutely clear: Roanoke was an unsuitable location because there was no sufficient harbor on the Outer Banks. This was known in England long before the failure of Lane's colony, because Grenville would have reported as much when he returned from depositing the colonists, and he carried a letter from Lane criticizing the harbors. This report must have been circulated; the need for a new location if another colony were to be tried was general knowledge by 1586.

Lane's reports on his return reiterated constantly how poor the site had been, possibly to forestall criticism of his leadership or the decision to return so hastily. In one account, he said the harbor had proven to be "naught," and wrote of his sense of shame when Drake arrived at "our bad harbor." Drake's experience of having to anchor far offshore also contributed to the consensus. Hariot, too, felt that the Outer Banks were perilous because they were so shallow and "full of dangerous flats." Even the Spanish relaxed; their intelligence report called the area "inhospitable" and went on, "The land itself would wage war against them! To say that they can maintain a base there from which to damage the fleets is idle talk."

No one could question that Roanoke was a bad choice of location; the real debate was over what any colony could actually contribute. Would it be a drain, something that required sustenance and produced little? For those who saw privateering as the main activity, a colony probably seemed a pure liability now. The dream of a plantation, even in a good location, being able to supply ships with food and facilities for repairs and refitting seemed very remote. The real question was whether colonies could produce something of their own valuable enough to justify the cost through the long foundation period. This debate began as soon as Grenville returned from depositing the colonists, as Lane's letters circulated among opinion makers.

All that was known before 1585 had come from the enthusiastic reports of Arthur Barlowe, who wrote of incredible abundance and rich commodities, but on the basis of little experience. With the Lane colony, the real testing began. The letters Lane sent back with Grenville were almost as hopeful as Barlowe's, saying that the commodities produced by all the countries of Europe did not equal those of Roanoke, and specifying exactly what the colony would be able to provide its English investors. Imagine the general chagrin when Lane returned the next year saying that the commodities there were not worth the fetching, something that others in England had already suspected. Lane reported that, since the harbor was no good for privateering, the only break that could make the colony successful was the discovery of gold or a passage through the continent to the Pacific. The mainland of North America was now seen as a barrier rather than a land of opportunity. He did go on to argue that if a mine or passage were found, then it would be worthwhile to develop the land itself, and he still believed it would be among the richest in the world. The new element was his perception that development of North America's potential would be a long and arduous task. No more was heard of rich products there for the picking up.

Thomas Hariot's assessment was more sober; he went to neither of Lane's extremes. Hariot argued consistently throughout his writings that North America, specifically the area around Roanoke, could produce many things Europe wanted and needed, and he never disguised the fact that hard work would be involved. What he had to say carried great weight because he alone had tested and gathered the flora and fauna of America; his was the word of a scientist against that of a soldier and adventurer. Lane endorsed his book in a preface, saying that Hariot was "an Actor in the Colony, or a man no less for his honesty than learning commendable: as that I dare boldly avouch it may very well pass with the credit of truth even among the most true relations of this age." Hariot's *Brief and True Report of the New Found Land of Virginia*, addressed as it was to "the Adventurers, Favorers, and Welwillers of the enterprise for the inhabiting and planting in Virginia," was a propaganda tract designed to attract investors to yet another attempt to found a colony. To call it a piece of propaganda is not to denigrate it; it was written with the goal of presenting the truth as he saw it, because he thought North America really was worth developing—for its own sake and not as an adjunct to privateering.

Hariot, like the others who wrote on America, included some purely conventional statements about the fruitfulness of the land; but most of what he wrote is remarkable because it clearly was grounded in his own experience. Rarely did he describe any product without authenticating his information by presenting the results of his experiments or his observations of native uses. There is a ring of truth about his book. Hariot stated at the outset that he was going to divide his description of what the land had to offer into three sections. One dealt with the sustenance of life, as he put it, the foods available. Another focused on materials for building, and that section gave him an opportunity to describe the landscape and counter the idea that it was a barren sandbar. The third category, and the one he placed first, was what he called "merchantable" commodities, those that could be developed for sale in England to reward people who invested in the colony. This section was, of course, the crucial one for deciding whether future colonization would be attempted.

Hariot's discussion of plants and animals available to feed colonists was a very full one, designed to refute those who claimed the settlers left in such haste with Drake because they were starving. Hariot asserted absolutely that no colony need starve. He began with foods actually cultivated by the Indians, of which the chief one was maize, "Indian corn." Hariot called it "Guinea wheat or Turkey wheat," indicating that he thought it originated in one of those exotic countries. He said it was the size and shape of English peas, but came in beautiful colors, white, red, yellow, and blue. He liked cornbread and thought maize could be used in brewing ale and beer. The greatest thing about corn, though, was its enormous yield and the great speed with which it came to maturity. Hariot wrote, "It is a grain of marvelous great increase." The versatility and pleasantness of corn were very important in Hariot's scheme, because he was forced to admit that the settlers' experiments with growing English grains were inconclusive. Some that had fallen casually on the ground grew well, but their main supplies were soaked with sea water when the *Tiger* ran aground and became musty and useless. Hariot was sure that English grains would do well, but maize would fill all a colony's needs until they were established.

In addition to maize, the Indians cultivated some vegetables that the English compared to peas and beans. The peas he preferred to English peas. These vegetables were also capable of many uses, and Hariot described the Indians' methods of preparing them. He also wrote about pumpkins, various squashes, and sunflowers, a "great herb, in form of a Marigold, about six foot in height, the head with the flower is a span in breadth." The Indians, he said, made both bread and broth of sunflower seeds. The cultivated plants were followed by Hariot's description of the wild plants and animals available to inhabitants. He was enthusiastic about the abundance of fowl and fish, and made clear that each season had its sources of food. He always noted Indian practices and especially reported what they said about how to find, identify, and prepare edible wild plants. Whether intentionally or not, his report provided powerful evidence that any colony would necessarily be reliant on the Indians for survival.

The section on "merchantable" commodities was the heart of Hariot's discussion, and he was careful to authenticate his assertions there. He thought he had seen many promising products for the textile industry, the most important industry in England. Investors hoped an American colony might produce types of cloth new to British manufacturers, especially silk. Hariot had found a kind of grass "upon the blades whereof there groweth very good silk in form of a thin glittering skin to be stripped off." Not only did he believe that it was similar to a grass from which silk was made in Persia, in the same latitude as Roanoke, but he said that the colonists had already had a piece of silk grosgrain made from it. He also thought the climate would be right for silkworms; in fact, he and other colonists thought they had seen silkworms as big as walnuts, but these were probably actually tent-caterpillars. Hariot believed that the area would also be good for flax and hemp, though he admitted he had not seen much growing wild.

There were other products for the English cloth industry as well. For instance, the colonists thought they had discovered a huge deposit of alum, important as a fixative for dyes, in the clay along the coasts. Hariot also assumed that many dyes could be found in America. He reported Indian use of various pigments for body paint or for dying animal skins and baskets, but cautiously said that their suitability for cloth had yet to be tested. He was sure they would be good for something, though. Whether the native dyes proved really worthwhile or not, Hariot asserted that European dyes such as woad could be grown profitably in America. Oils for soap manufacture were another potential bonanza for textile manufacturers. Hariot reported that walnuts and acorns were plentiful and that the Indians extracted oil from them; he also thought bear fat would be useful, because it was virtually liquid. Finally, Hariot briefly mentioned the possibilities in fur and deerskin trading, though he made it clear that his own experience in this area was sketchy.

Hariot was enthusiastic about the possibility of importing medicines from America and believed that he had seen examples comparable to expensive drugs imported from southern and eastern countries. In addition to sassafras, Hariot thought there were several "sweet gums" and "other Apothecary drugs" that would prove to be effective medicines and important sources of revenue to future colonies; but he restricted his claims until they were tested and researched by "men of skill in that kind." Hariot said his samples had been lost, probably in their hasty departure.

The *Brief and True Report* soft-pedaled claims about minerals, which had figured so heavily in the writings of others. Hariot claimed the "mineral man" had found iron that he thought could be developed, especially given the plentiful supply of wood to fuel the furnaces. The settlers had heard reports of copper and silver and had seen Indians wearing jewelry of these metals, but Hariot was very cautious in his claims. He had seen pearls; in fact he said that members of the company sometimes found them while eating mussels, though they were not of good quality. One man had gathered five thousand pearls from the Indians and had selected enough for a "fair chain" for Queen Elizabeth, but it had been tossed overboard with the other things by the sailors in their haste to leave.

In addition to the things Hariot had personally seen and tested, he argued that many other rich commodities would be possible in Roanoke. They had seen big "luscious sweet" grapes and he was sure that with proper tending the vines would enable the colonists to make good wine. Hariot also argued from the latitude of the colony that it should be able to produce anything grown in southern Spain or even North Africa. The colonists had brought sugar canes from the West Indies, but the plants died on the voyage. Since the time of year had proved to be wrong for planting anyway, he felt that hopes for sugar production were still open. It was clear to Hariot that all kinds of citrus fruits should grow in these latitudes as well. The fact that all these plants did not presently grow there was not proof that they would not. In fact, the promoters knew that Spain had introduced many of these same crops into islands in its empire; there were good precedents for expecting such experiments to be successful. It would take much more experience before colonial promoters came to realize fully that it was impossible to predict the climates of areas in North America simply by extrapolation from regions in the same latitude in the Old World. Semitropical fruits continued to be planted, and to die, in southern colonies for decades to come.

Ironically, the great cash crop of the Virginia colony founded in 1607, the product that finally made a colony pay its way, was not mentioned by Hariot in his list of "merchantable" commodities. Tobacco, which Hariot himself greatly enjoyed, appeared in the *Brief and True Report* in a discussion of the foods used by the Indians. Hariot gave full instructions for growing, processing, and smoking it. He described its

use in Indian religious rites, and gave his opinion that it was a very
effective medicine for a variety of ills, but he never guessed that it
would be the most lucrative crop produced in any southern mainland
colony in the seventeenth century.

Of all those concerned in the Roanoke colony, Hariot was most realistic in his thinking; he and the Hakluyts agreed about the role
colonies should play in English policy. The Hakluyts had always seen
the aim of aiding privateering as a chimera. They did not know that it
was impossible, but they feared diverting attention toward a short-
term, self-limiting goal and away from the much more important
contribution colonies could make to England. Hariot agreed with them
and added the weight of his experience in America to their arguments.
These scientifically inclined men were thinking of long-range prospects, of developing, possibly over several years, the potential of America. Their position was extremely difficult, because as long as people
went to the New World expecting quick and easy wealth, either from
privateering or by acquiring precious metals and gems, no one would
be willing to put in the hard work and money necessary to make
colonies succeed. On the other hand, the argument had to be stated
delicately because some sort of return had to be promised or investment
money would not be forthcoming.

The reader can see Hariot struggling to maintain all these arguments in some sort of equilibrium without doing violence to the truth.
He did not foreclose the possibility of mineral wealth, and suggested
that it would be more likely farther inland, and he argued that semitropical plants would grow in North Carolina. But he lavished most
attention on those products that he had personally researched and
tested, and he bolstered his reasoning by pointing out that already established English industries had need of these commodities. Throughout
his book Hariot returned again and again to his themes, all of which
centered on the need to *develop* the true potential of America. He frequently suggested that experts must be sent to do the final testing and
planning for product development, and just as frequently pointed to
the resident experts, the Indians, as the best possible guides to the
commodities of America.

What Hariot and the Hakluyts had in mind was a very modern concept of empire. They hoped the colony would be able to provide all
those necessities that England then bought from other European coun-

tries. The position could be explosive; England's textile industry, central to its economy, could not function without oil and dyes, but many of these had to be bought from southern European countries, all potential enemies. Spain and England were currently involved in a raging sea war; France and England had been at war off and on for centuries. What it all amounted to was a stranglehold on the English economy at the whim of other countries. England could not be a great nation until it achieved independence guaranteed by a steady and reliable source of its economic necessities.

Woad, alum, medicinal earths, and oil were not as glamorous as gold and silver, but the Hakluyts and Hariot were determined to prove that they could be more worthwhile. England had no need to remain parasitic on the great Spanish empire; commodities like these would build a greater English empire, one that would last because it would be based on self-renewing resources. It was in this spirit that those who supported development of indigenous products argued that America would contribute "infinite commodities."

Not only would the colonies supply British industries, according to this argument, but they would also constitute a major market for the finished products. The English economy would be revitalized by the demands of American consumers. The "naked savages" would particularly welcome English woolen cloth, but all inhabitants of America would need goods of European manufacture. The patriotic fervor in these men was as great as it was in those who saw colonies as a way to strike an immediate blow against Spain. They foresaw the British Empire as a single closed economic unit; England could then stand up to any enemy without fear. Such was the implicit promise held out to future investors by Hariot and the Hakluyts, and it must have seemed a powerful inducement. It was enough to lure a new group of investors to try once again with the final Roanoke colony.

In the conclusion to the *Brief and True Report*, Hariot asserted that the possibilities he described were just a fraction of those existing on the east coast of North America. The colonists' incursions into the mainland had convinced him that it was infinitely richer than the islands of the Outer Banks, and he pointed out that the Spaniards had originally found rather poor islands in the east and had then discovered untold riches as they moved west. It was logical to assume that the same might happen to the English. He believed the Indians further inland might be more highly developed than those the colonists had met, an idea also suggested by the Spanish example. To clinch his arguments, he again pointed to the latitude of Roanoke, corresponding to "the Island of Japan, the land of China, Persia, Turkey, the Islands of Cyprus and Candy, the South parts of Greece, Italy, and Spain, and of many other notable and famous countries." A colony in the same latitude ought to be able to produce what those countries produced.

The best way to understand America's potential, according to Hariot's reasoning, was to study Indian methods of cultivation, processing, and use. Instead of seeing them as at best irrelevant and at worst dangerous to the colonial effort, as most colonists and promoters had done, the Hakluyts and Hariot understood that the Indians were in the profoundest sense crucial to the whole enterprise. They were immediately crucial in a way that even Ralph Lane could grasp in that they kept the colonists alive with their surplus food, but those who favored development of American commodities realized that dependence on the Indians was fundamental.

How did the Indians stand in English estimation after a year of mutual experience? Important changes had taken place in perceptions of the potential relationship of American natives to future colonies. It was more difficult to hold the simpleminded idea that the Indians would recognize European superiority and voluntarily give up their culture and sovereignty in order to secure its benefits. Many people, particularly those who were less intimately involved in the Lane colony's experience, did continue to think in this comfortable way, however. This easy belief may have been bolstered by shortsighted people who suppressed reports of unpleasant incidents such as Amadas's encounter on Chesapeake Bay in 1584. Some of Lane's cruelty to the Indians may also have been silently censored, which meant that the next group of colonists would have had less than realistic expectations about their possible relationship with the Americans around them. Such tailoring of accounts, though understandable, was sure to create problems in the long run because of the false hopes it generated.

Though the official line continued to be that the Indians would welcome and aid English colonists, there is some evidence that behind-the-scenes discussion was more realistic. Hariot's *Brief and True Report* was published after the final group had left for Roanoke, and he made a point of saying that they had been supplied with enough food to last until next year's arrival of the supply ships. Independence of Indian aid was apparently being sought, though of course any veteran colonist knew how many possible accidents could rob a party of self-reliance.

Hariot's book subtly showed how the situation had changed in Indian-English relations. Though he blamed clashes on the colonists' harshness, he offered advice for coping with the changed situation. His argument was that the Indians could still be brought "to fear and love us," but that redoubled vigilance would now be necessary. Hariot trod a fine line between his assertion that Indian hostility did not make colonization too dangerous and his belief that the settlement must make a consistent show of military preparedness and determination. He still believed that mutual love and respect were possible if the colony's leaders would insist on "good government"; that is, if they would keep the rank and file under control. There was a chilling change in the younger Richard Hakluyt's point of view, though. He was apparently deeply disturbed by the hostility shown Lane's colony, so much so that he recommended sending veterans of the cruel and bloody continental wars to discipline those "stubborn Savages as shall refuse obedience to her Majestie." He was now willing to force conformity, rather than to win it by the loving kindess he had earlier advocated.

The final party of colonists associated with the Roanoke ventures involved a totally new organization and set of intentions. The colony that left England for America in 1587 was much more knowledgeable, though the vast majority of them were emigrating for the first time; but they also had a very different situation to deal with than had earlier parties. There would be no grace period during which Indians and English would learn about each other. Each side thought it knew very well the values and intentions of the other. Though the final colony was completely different in goals and personnel, it carried the legacy of Lane's military colony and the privateering connection on its back. That inheritance haunted all the efforts associated with this colony and eventually destroyed it.

7

A GENUINE SETTLEMENT

MUCH had changed by the time the third and final expedition was set for Roanoke in 1587. The problems encountered and generated by Lane's colony had dampened the easy enthusiasm of many potential backers and friends of the venture. The withdrawal of Sir Francis Walsingham meant loss of an important voice at court. The clear failure to establish a refitting base for privateers, or even to find a suitable location for such a base, alienated many wealthy men and made others doubtful of the colony's possible value, especially as no precious metals had been found, and development of other resources appeared to be a long, laborious task. Disaffection had shown up as early as 1586, when there had been trouble getting investors for the relief voyage to Lane's colony. Several promoters were issued letters of reprisal in 1587, which meant they were sending out expeditions, but efforts to link any of these with a new Roanoke venture apparently failed.

Even Raleigh, whose situation was changing by 1587, began to pull back. He had put a great deal of money, his own and others', into American colonization and did not feel able to keep up that level of commitment. One contemporary said the colony had already absorbed as much as £30,000, a very great fortune. There had been returns, but all from privateering, and the colony had made no contribution to that income. Raleigh had also stretched his political capital in working for the colony, sometimes seizing men and supplies in peremptory ways; he could not draw indefinitely on his influence at court to protect him. Nor was his position with the queen safe; the beautiful young Earl of Essex had appeared at court by 1587, and he, not Raleigh, now seemed to be the royal favorite. Raleigh's presence was still important to Elizabeth, but he was no longer pre-eminent among her followers.

Only one person seems to have been wholeheartedly convinced that the effort must go on—the painter John White. He devoted himself to gathering support for another expedition, and, when it did embark, he went along as its governor. White was to preside over a colony different in every way from its predecessor. Instead of a company of young men with military experience, his group was composed of families, which meant that the colonists would come to America prepared to stay, not expecting to be rotated home in a year or two. Whereas the earlier colony had been designed to support privateering, the emphasis in White's colony was on agricultural self-sufficiency and development of American products for English markets. In place of the Lane colony's hierarchical, authoritarian structure under the single figure of Raleigh in England, this new venture was organized as a corporation in which the colonists themselves took a leading role. They were to be responsible for their own destinies and were to profit directly from their own efforts.

White's colony was intended to settle, not at Roanoke, but in Chesapeake Bay, the region all experienced hands agreed was superior to the Carolina Outer Banks. White himself may have accompanied Lane's expedition there and therefore may have had firsthand knowledge of the area. Had these plans been carried out, the colony would probably have been located near where Jamestown was founded in 1607. There is some evidence that Raleigh continued to hope that a separate privateering base could still be constructed on the coast once the main colony was well established.

The colony sent to Roanoke in 1587 under the governorship of John White represented, in fact, the prototype of all later successful plantations. None succeeded without following this model; and yet this colony failed because the legacy of Roanoke's past was too powerful to be overcome. Its failure meant that later colonial promoters did not realize clearly which of Roanoke's mistakes had been the fatal ones. Many of the same mistakes were made over again at Jamestown, the first permanent colony, at the price of very great suffering before it moved to the successful, family-centered model.

John White took the initiative in gathering together a group of settlers willing to go to America on the new terms he outlined. These must have been people with a little bit of capital to invest, at least to the extent of helping to outfit themselves. Only two other men who had already served in Roanoke were willing to return, but White must have been a very persuasive figure to have assembled the group he did. He claimed to have one hundred fifty people willing to go; ultimately one hundred ten were deposited at Roanoke. This body of colonists hammered out an agreement with Raleigh in which each man was guaranteed at least five hundred acres of land in return for investing his person even if he had no money to invest, and families were to receive even more.

The City of Raleigh, as the new corporation and colony was to be called, was under the direction of Governor John White and his twelve assistants, the board of directors. Under this system, the governor was expected to consult the assistants on all important questions, but decision-making power rested with him. Perhaps nothing demonstrates so clearly the changed nature of the enterprise as the grant of arms to the corporation and its officers. Gone were the gentleman-soldiers who led the first colony, yet so strong was the Elizabethan assumption that such a venture must be led by people of high social standing that Raleigh apparently pulled strings to have certificates of gentle status conferred on the officers of his corporation regardless of their origins. Usually, one can tell a good deal about a person's antecedents by reading the heraldic meaning of his coat of arms, but so ersatz were these grants that almost nothing can be gleaned from them. John White's, for example, gives no evidence about his past or origins. Of the twelve, only White and Simon Fernandes were identified in the grant as gentlemen. For the others, the conferring of coats of arms must have been rather cynical, an impression strengthened by the fact that the Garter King of Arms, who created the elaborate designs, in some cases left the names blank to be filled in later. No research can have been done on the background or claims of these men, and the heraldry of their arms would have been meaningless. One of the twelve assistants granted a coat of arms was Ananias Dare, a tiler and bricklayer, who had recently married Eleanor, John White's daughter, and who was soon to be the father of Virginia Dare.

A certain amount can be learned from White's own list of the colonists. Judging by coincidence of names, there were fourteen families. Four of the families included a mother, father, and child; one child was so young that he was still being nursed by his mother. Two of the women, Margaret Harvie and Eleanor Dare, were so far advanced

in pregnancy that their deliveries occurred soon after arrival in
Roanoke. Six were married couples without children, and four were
fathers and sons who probably expected to be joined by the rest of their
families in future voyages. George Howe, one of the assistants, came
with his son George. The boy was left an orphan when his father was
killed by Indians shortly after their arrival in Roanoke. Nine children
came overall, all boys, and seventeen women. Seven of the women and
three of the boys came without any apparent family attachments; they
were probably servants, as were James Hynde and William Clement,
who had been released from Colchester Castle where they had been
jailed for stealing. The rest of the one hundred ten colonists were men
alone. Most of the emigrants, because their names are so common and
their places of origin unknown, cannot be traced.[1]

The colonists joined White in London in early spring, 1587. They
boarded their three small ships—the *Lion,* a ship of 120 tons with
Simon Fernandes as its master, a flyboat that was smaller than the
flagship, and a small pinnace, commanded by Captain Edward
Stafford—and went round to Portsmouth in early April, to the Isle of
Wight, and then to Plymouth, finally sailing for America on May 8th.
This was a late start, and the delay would have consumed provisions
intended for the colonists' use in America. The reason for the long
wait is unknown. All expeditions went south to catch the trade winds,
making landfall first in the West Indies and then proceeding up the
coast; but the voyage was very long in this case, just ten days short of
three months, further consuming provisions.

Life at sea was miserable at best in the late sixteenth century. Only
the highest officers had bunks; passengers and crew simply found a spot
between decks and rolled up in a blanket. If the weather was very nice,
they might sleep on deck. Food was cooked on a fire built in the forward section between decks on sand or rock ballast with the smoke
vented through a pipe. Typical rations were salt beef, pork, and fish
with biscuit, hardtack that became so hard that it had to be broken up
with a mallet or, if it got wet, was moldy and maggoty. There were
barrels of beer and water, and the passengers and crew also received
oatmeal, cheese, and butter. After the first four weeks, typically, the
beer, water, and beef began to deteriorate; water, at least, would be
replenished in the West Indies.

If the ship ran into storms, then life became truly miserable, and the later the expedition remained in the West Indies the more probable this became. The ship inevitably leaked fairly heavily in a storm, and the passengers were forced to remain in the almost unventilated area between decks, where the bilge water would become mixed with their vomit, feces, and urine. As the pumps fell behind in their efforts, the stench, horrifying in the best conditions, quickly became overpowering. Cockroaches and rats, stirred up by the ship's motion and the rolling water, further discomfited the company. Such was the life that seamen had learned to endure; it must have been difficult in the extreme for the colonists in their small ships, particularly the women with children and those who were heavily pregnant.[2]

The sole account of this expedition is the journal kept by John White. From its earliest pages, there is a litany of accusations against Simon Fernandes. White had been one of the faction in 1585 that accused the Portuguese pilot of having endangered the fleet and run the *Tiger* aground through carelessness. Before the colony left European waters Fernandes had resumed his malicious practices, according to the governor, "lewdly" abandoning the flyboat in hopes that its complement of colonists would not be able to find the way to North America. The smaller ship did arrive at Roanoke virtually simultaneously with the flagship, and White portrayed the Portuguese as greatly vexed by that. Why he would have wanted to endanger the entire enterprise by such a maneuver White never made clear, nor does it make sense, since the homeward voyage would be both safer and potentially more profitable with two good-sized ships. A single ship was almost useless for privateering.

The real contention between White and Fernandes was over privateering. Fernandes was one of the assistants, though he was not intended to stay in America, and he surely wanted the colony to succeed. But his interest was in privateering and in using the colony as a base, so he saw no reason why this voyage should not spend some time chasing ships in the West Indies as all the others had done. The governor worried about the effect the delay would have on some of the passengers and was understandably afraid of engaging in full-scale battle with another ship, with the possibility of death, injury, or enslavement for all concerned. We do not know Fernandes' version of events, but White was sure he was playing with the colony's fate. White was nominally over Fernandes, but in reality he was not a strong commander and was unable to do more than fume and complain. Frustration may account for the outlandish quality of some of his claims.[3]

The governor wrote almost nothing about the Atlantic crossing. His narration began with their anchorage off St. Croix on June 22nd, 6½ weeks after setting out. They stayed there three days and some of the colonists had their first experience of the dangers of an alien land. After eating a small fruit that resembled green apples, their mouths began to burn and their tongues swelled so that some of them could not speak. The nursing infant was similarly affected by his mother's milk. The effect, though very painful, wore off the next day. Because they found no running fresh water, several colonists drank from a standing pond whose water poisoned them. Those who washed in it found their faces so swollen that they could not see for five or six days. Luckily, a search party found a spring of clear water running from a high rock and five giant tortoises to eat, so large that sixteen men had difficulty in carrying one. The explorers also spotted some Indians, and White was furious because Fernandes had assured him the island was uninhabited. In his mind, it was just one more instance of the pilot's lack of concern for the colonists.

From St. Croix they went on to Puerto Rico, where they took on fresh water. White again believed they had been misdirected; he said they consumed more beer during the three days they were there than they gained in water. Beer was not all that was lost. Two colonists, both Irish, apparently deserted on Puerto Rico, the kind of incident that confirmed the constant suspicion of foreigners, particularly Roman Catholics, characteristic of most English people in this period. One of these men, Darby Glande or Glavin, may have been deserting his own wife as well as the colony in general; one of the women was listed as Elizabeth Glane. Glavin had been in Roanoke already with Lane's colony; he told the Spanish that he had been on a French ship captured by Grenville and was forced to become a colonist. He claimed his participation in White's colony had also been against his will. When he was captured, he warned the governor of Puerto Rico of an impending attack by privateering vessels being sent from England; despite his cooperation, however, he was sent to work as a galley slave in Havana. The loss of his experience was serious for the colonists.

Further attempts to collect supplies on Puerto Rico came to nothing; White attributed their failures to "our Simon's" malevolence. They had intended to take on salt, essential for preserving food, at Rojo Bay where the Spanish had a stockpile. As soon as the pinnace was readied with a heavily armed complement of men, Fernandes suddenly changed his mind and said it was not safe. White described a comic-opera charade in which the Portuguese, claiming the ship was in danger, "suddenly began to swear, and tear God in pieces," pulling away from the anchorage. Fernandes may have been remembering the previous expedition when Lane had been sent by Grenville to take on salt and had been furious that he and his men had been placed in such danger.

White had also planned to pick up young orange, pineapple, banana, and mammee apple plants for culture in Roanoke. He had made drawings of these in 1585 and believed he knew just where to find them near the shore. Again Fernandes said such a stop was impossible, and he offered to get plant specimens as well as cattle on the island of Hispaniola, where he had contacts. When they reached Hispaniola, on July 4th, it became apparent, according to White, that Fernandes had never intended to stop there. He sailed past the place where his friend, a Frenchman named Alençon, lived. When White asked him if it was not time to land, Simon answered that they had already gone too far; and besides, Sir Walter Raleigh had told him that the King of Spain had captured Alençon and taken him into Spain, so he was probably dead. They made one last try to take on salt in the Caicos Island group, but found none. White, in a passage filled with innuendo, said that Fernandes "solaced himself ashore, with one of the company, in part of the Island," while the colonists desperately sought the salt pans or hunted for fresh meat. They found no salt but did catch many swans. Their consolation now was that the next land they saw would be Virginia.

The little fleet came to an anchorage off the Outer Banks on July 16th at what Fernandes took to be Croatoan Island. After two or three days, he realized he was mistaken and moved up the coast. The ships were almost wrecked on Cape Lookout, a disaster prevented, according to White, by the greater vigilance of Captain Stafford, master of their pinnace, "such was the carelessness and ignorance of our Master." Finally, on July 22nd, the ships anchored off Roanoke. White went immediately aboard the pinnace, which was suited for maneuvering in shallow coastal waters, with forty "of his best men" to seek out the holding party of fifteen left by Grenville. He expected to learn from them about the "state of the Country" and relations with the Indians, then to return immediately to the ships and move on to the intended site of the new colony, Chesapeake Bay. He pointed out that he had written orders from Raleigh to do just that.

To the governor's horror, as soon as the pinnace began to move away from the *Lion,* "a Gentleman" who was a confederate of Fernandes' called out to the mariners that they should not bring any of the forty back again, but deposit them at Roanoke. Only White and two or three others were to be allowed back on board the *Lion.* The reason given for this mutiny was that "the Summer was far spent"; it was the high season for privateering, and Fernandes and all the sailors were anxious to get back to the West Indies. The expectation, built up over so many voyages, that a trip to Roanoke meant an opportunity for privateering now began to plague the colony and ultimately led to its loss. When White discovered that the ships' companies were entirely behind Fernandes, he gave way.

White was apparently no leader himself. His complaints were intended to hide his inability to exercise the control that nominally was his as governor of the fleet and colony. He may also have been happier to be back on familiar ground at Roanoke despite its inadequacy as a site and even despite the bad relations the Lane colony had generated with the neighboring Indians. It was well known that the Chesapeake Bay Indians were more highly organized and more warlike than those of the Carolina Outer Banks. Fernandes, with his previous experience in Chesapeake Bay in the Spanish service and knowing of the extermination of the Jesuits sent there in the early 1570s as well as the attack on Amadas in 1584, may have been partly motivated by a desire to protect the colonists. Confusion over motives is deepened considerably by the fact that, though White portrayed Fernandes as a malicious and greedy man dumping the colonists to run off privateering, the fleet actually stayed at Roanoke with the settlers more than a month, until the very end of August. This discrepancy was never explained.

Governor White's willingness to remain at Roanoke may have been strengthened the next day when he and some of the men went to the north part of the island, to the area inhabited by the Lane colony.

They found that, though the earthworks surrounding the fort were "razed down," the fort building inside them and the houses nearby were all standing. Their lower stories were overgrown with melon vines on which deer were grazing, but only minor repairs were required. White immediately set the men to work cleaning up the existing houses and building additional cottages. Apparently each family was to have its own residence. On July 25th, the boat lost off Portugal arrived with the rest of the colonists, "to the great joy, and comfort of the whole company," and to the consternation, White reported, of Fernandes. The colony was now complete.

There was one ominous note among all the hopeful portents: no sign was found of the fifteen men left behind by Grenville, except for a skeleton they took to be the bones of one of them. The implication of Indian hostility was strengthened when, six days after their arrival, George Howe, one of the assistants, was killed by unidentified Indians. White was not sure whether they had come over to Roanoke Island because they knew of the English arrival or to hunt the plentiful deer. The circumstances in which they encountered Howe indicate that the colonists were taking no precautions. He was two miles away from the others, wading in shallow water "almost naked, without any weapon." He had been catching crabs with a small forked stick when he was attacked. White reported that the Indians gave him many wounds and mutilated his head after death; his son George was now alone. The attacking Indians returned to the mainland before the encounter was discovered.

The colonists had reason to hope for good relations with at least some of the Indians, however. Manteo had gone back to England with Lane's colony, and he was to be a source of strength and aid to the colonists with whom he had now returned to America; another Indian, Towaye, was also with White's colony. At the end of July Manteo and several of the colonists under Captain Stafford went by water to Croatoan Island, Manteo's home. White said that the purpose of the visit was to learn what kind of treatment they could expect from the Indians around Roanoke and "to renew our old friendship with them." They also hoped to learn about the fate of Grenville's holding party. Despite their friendly intentions, the colonists approached the Croatoan Indians with their guns drawn. At first they thought a Croatoan attack was being contemplated, but the Indians fled at the sight of

English muskets. When Manteo called out to them in their own language, they threw away their bows and arrows and returned to embrace the party.

However friendly in outward signs this initial meeting was, there were already undercurrents of tension. The Croatoans wanted to draw up guidelines from the beginning. As they embraced the English, they asked them "not to gather or spill any of their corn, for that they had but little." These Indians were not prepared to have the colony press them for food through the winter. Stafford answered that he and the settlers had no intention of asking anything but friendship from the Croatoans; the colony was to live alongside them "as brethren, and friends." At this answer, the Indians invited the company to a celebration, where the English were feasted "after their manner."

Still the underlying tension was there. At the feast, the Croatoans asked for some form of badge or sign they might show to indicate their friendly status to any English people they encountered. Several of them had been hurt, they said, by Lane's colonists because they lacked such a token, including one man, now lame, who was exhibited to Stafford and his men. The Croatoan leaders quickly moved to smooth over the social breach, saying they knew Lane's men had mistaken them for Wingina's Indians and therefore were not to blame. But they were quietly insistent on rules of conduct as they once again began a relationship with an English colony. Next time, they might not be willing to excuse such a disastrous case of mistaken identity. White did not say whether the settlers tried to give them such a badge or token.

The party spent the night with Manteo's kin. Next day, the colonists asked how Indians on the mainland were disposed to the renewed settlement, particularly in the towns of Secoton, Aquascogoc, and Pomeiooc. Stafford asked the Croatoans to assure them that the English came in peace and friendship, suggesting that "all unfriendly dealings past on both parts should be utterly forgiven and forgotten"; the Indians agreed to do their best. They would try to bring the leaders of these towns, or their answers, to Roanoke in one week's time. But they also made the English understand that tension and hostility existed and could not easily be erased. They confirmed that George Howe had been killed by some of Wingina's men and that the party included Wanchese, the Indian originally taken to England with Manteo.

This was chilling news, because it made clear how rare a convert like Manteo was. The English had always told themselves that their culture was so clearly superior to that of the Indians that the Americans would quickly and easily give up their own ways, that the process of conversion to "civility and Christianity" would happen naturally. In fact, though the Indians borrowed some artifacts from the Europeans, especially those like metal tools that made their own activities easier, they were not at all convinced of the superiority of European culture. As they looked at the relative helplessness of the English in Roanoke, they judged otherwise.

Not only had Howe been killed by Roanoke Indians, but the colonists learned that Grenville's holding party had also been dispersed by an alliance of the three towns. The story confirmed English assumptions about human relations; the men had been living "carelessly" and were therefore vulnerable, and the Indians had attacked by treachery and stealth. The story was as follows: about thirty Indians approached the village, most hiding behind trees. Since they could see only eleven of the fifteen men, they sent two emissaries to approach the settlement and ask for a parley. The two ambassadors appeared to be unarmed, so the English sent out two unarmed men to talk to them. As they were embracing, one of the pair took out a wooden sword from under his mantel and killed one of the English with a blow to the head. Then the other Indians came out of hiding and began to attack. The unharmed English delegate ran back to the storehouse where the food and ammunition were kept; but the Indians set it on fire, and all the soldiers ran out in disorder with whatever weapons they could snatch up. The fighting went on about an hour. One more man was killed on each side before the English, many of whom were wounded, finally escaped to their boat. They managed to pick up the four men who had been gathering oysters about a quarter mile away and then rowed to a little island between Port Lane and Port Ferdinando. After a while, they left and were never heard of again.

Grenville's men had had no way of knowing about events in the Lane colony just before its end, but White apparently blamed them for their fate. They had lived "carelessly" in a situation where extreme caution and constant show of force were necessary, according to English common sense. Their story made frighteningly clear the situation the new colonists were facing. Not only were the Indians on the mainland, led by the Roanokes, apparently implacably hostile, but the conditions favored them. The encounter had been carried on in thick woods with the nimble Indians hiding behind trees to shoot their arrows. In these circumstances, the muskets of which the English were so proud were a liability, turning the soldiers into standing targets.

Seven days passed, and no representatives of the mainland tribes appeared. At midnight on August 8th, White, having decided that he could delay his revenge for George Howe and the Grenville party no longer, secretly went with Captain Stafford, commander of the pinnace, and twenty-four men to the mainland to prepare an attack. Manteo was one of the company, and White said he "behaved himself toward us as a most faithful English man." He acted as guide and interpreter. Early in the morning of August 9th, they silently approached the village of Dasemunkepeuc, Roanoke's headquarters. They saw some people sitting around their fire and attacked without warning. "The miserable souls herewith amazed fled into a place of thick reeds growing fast by." The soldiers, having killed one, pursued the others into the weeds to "acquit their evil doing towards us." But this was not the revenge they sought, because these were not the offending Indians. Precisely what the Croatoans feared had come to pass; these were friendly Indians from that tribe who, hearing that Wingina's Roanokes had fled, came to their village to gather their corn, tobacco, and fruit.

Slowly White began to realize the enormity of what the colonists had done in their surprise attack. The people sitting around the fire had included women and children as well as men. White tried to explain, saying that Indian men and women dressed so much alike that it was impossible to distinguish them, particularly in the still-dark morning. As it was, a *werowance's* wife was saved only because she was carrying a child on her back. One man escaped by running up to Captain Stafford calling him by name. It was a sad day for the colony. Not only had they again offended their only friends, but they had failed to teach their enemies that they could not attack the English with impunity. The war party gathered all the ripe corn, pumpkins, peas, and tobacco and returned to Roanoke, bringing with them the Croatoans including the *werowance* and his wife and child.

Manteo was a man caught between two cultures; his position was extremely painful. Having cast his lot with the English, he apparently now felt he had no choice but to go on supporting them. Governor

White said he was "somewhat grieved" by this unprovoked attack on his tribe, yet he accepted that it was the victims' own fault because they had failed to communicate with the colony at the end of a week as agreed. Manteo's position was formalized a few days later when he was baptized at Roanoke and given the title of Lord of Roanoke and Dasemunkepeuc "in reward of his faithful service." This ceremony had been planned before the expedition left England; White said that it was performed on Sir Walter Raleigh's orders. Raleigh's intention was apparently to install Manteo as a sort of feudal lord under him. Since he expected White's colonists to settle on Chesapeake Bay, Raleigh wanted Manteo to maintain the title to his territory to the south until he was again ready to set up a base in the region.

The ceremony and the new title probably meant something quite different to Manteo. Finding an Indian with whom they could establish a relationship and then designating him a lord or chief was a favorite European technique in the New World. It was much simpler to work through such a person than to attempt to understand the actual native power structure, but the effect was not always as anticipated. Frequently people who were willing to accept such a relationship were those who were already somewhat marginal to their own culture or, like Manteo, were made marginal through kidnapping and indoctrination. In these cases their ability to speak for their own tribes was doubtful.

Manteo, however, was an important person in his tribe at the time he was captured; his mother was probably chief of the Croatoans. They may have continued to tolerate the colonists far longer than they would have because of Manteo's presence among them, and they probably reaped benefits from the situation. The Croatoans may have been glad to have their own interpretation of events, especially the actions of other tribes, always immediately presented to the settlers. With an observer present in the colony, they could also keep track of English plans and actions and make their own plans accordingly. It is highly doubtful that Manteo was the simple tool White and the others thought he was. For the Croatoans his position with the colonists may have been simply an extension of the time-honored practice of placing members of the chief's family in other villages to control relationships.

Virginia Dare was born on August 18th; her name signified that she was the first English child born in the New World. Governor White was justifiably proud of his granddaughter as he recorded her christening on August 24th. Margaret Harvie's child was born sometime after that. Joy at the successful deliveries must have been clouded by increasing sounds of the fleet's preparations for departure. Once all the supplies were unloaded, the ballast was removed so the holds could be "rummaged," cleaned and washed down with vinegar to remove the smell and accumulated slime. White said the ships were also newly caulked. The sailors began to load fresh water and wood; as the fleet prepared, the settlers also were at work writing letters and preparing "tokens" for friends and family back in England.

As the time of departure neared, the colonists became fearful. They wanted at least two of the assistants to return to England to act as their agents, to ensure that they would not be forgotten or put at the bottom of the company's list of priorities. Three of the original council of assistants had remained in England when the fleet sailed, presumably to act in the colonists' interests; but now the anxious settlers wanted men there who knew their situation precisely. Panic may have been generated by their realization that even friendly Indians would not feed them as they had the Lane colony. White said that one assistant agreed to return, but the colonists insisted there be two. With "much persuading" he got Christopher Cooper to agree to go, but by the next day Cooper had changed his mind back again and wanted to stay with his "familiar friends."

Finally all the men, planters and assistants, went to White and asked him to be their agent in England. They argued that he could gather supplies better than anyone else. He refused, saying he would be accused of deserting the people whom he personally had persuaded to come. Those who were his and the colony's enemies would say he had gone to America "but politicly" to lead others astray. There was another worry in White's mind: despite his affection for the colonists, he did not trust them. He was worried that if they moved from Roanoke up to Chesapeake Bay as they were planning, all his belongings would either be left behind and ruined, or some of his possessions might be "pilfered." He claimed that when he had left the colony for only three days, he had returned to find some of his things missing.

Next day, the settlers renewed their pleas, and this time the women added their voices. They promised to sign a bond guaranteeing the

safeguarding of his possessions if he would return to England on their
behalf. The document, which White reproduced in full, made it abundantly clear that he had been importuned by them to leave America
and had agreed reluctantly. He was thus fully protected against
charges of desertion. The colonists spoke of "our known, and apparent
lacks, and needs" and affirmed their belief that White was the best man
to "labor, and take pains" in their behalf. They detailed his many
refusals to be their delegate to England and their more urgent
insistence that he should be.

Once he had agreed to go, White had just half a day to get ready; he
boarded the flyboat at midnight on August 27th. The homeward journey was marred from the beginning; twelve of the crew were injured by
the capstan, the revolving drum around which the cable was wound to
raise the anchor. The capstan was turned manually by rods or bars pro-
truding from it. On White's ship, one of the bars broke and the
tightly wound drum was released, so the other bars swung around and
struck the men fiercely. Though some of the sailors were so badly
injured that they never fully recovered, they tried again to raise the
anchor but were too weak and the same accident occurred again. There
was no recourse but to cut the cable and leave the anchor behind. This
was a very inauspicious beginning; the ship had a tiny crew, only
fifteen men in all, and now most of them were injured. Only five were
capable of full duties.

Nonetheless, the flyboat kept up with Simon Fernandes' flagship
until they arrived at the Azores, where Fernandes remained in hopes of
capturing some rich prizes. The undermanned flyboat was sent to England, apparently partly because of White's sense of urgency about gathering fresh supplies for the colonists. It was to be some time before
they were to see home, though. For twenty days they drifted aimlessly
because of "scarce and variable winds," alarmed because leaks in the
barrels had almost completely depleted their supply of fresh water.
Then a storm that raged for six days rose out of the northeast; the ship
was driven so far by the storm that they did not know where they were
and despaired of recovering their former position in less than two
weeks. Conditions were terrible: the sailors began to fall sick and two
died, they had nothing to drink but "stinking water, dregs of beer, and
lees of wine," which altogether made only three gallons, and "therefore
now we expected nothing but by famine to perish at sea."

Miraculously, they found themselves near land, but they had no idea of what country it might be until they went into a harbor and were approached by a small boat from another pinnace anchored there. They learned they were in the West of Ireland and were provided with fresh water, wine, and meat from the pinnace, which was English. The crew's troubles were not over; three more men died, and three others were taken off, too sick to continue. White transferred to another ship, the *Monkey,* as it left for England, leaving the flyboat and its crew behind. When he arrived at Southampton, White found that the flagship had been there for three weeks already. Fernandes had had an equally unfortunate voyage. Not only had he not captured any Spanish treasure, but his crew had been so overcome by sickness, possibly a tropical fever, that many had died, some of the leading men among them, and the rest had been so weak they had been unable to bring the ship into the harbor. They had been forced to drop their anchor outside and then were too feeble to raise it again, so that, had not a small bark happened to run across them, they might all have died where they were. Once again, though these misfortunes had nothing to do with the colony, backers in England would have seen Roanoke performing badly as a base for privateering.

8

ABANDONMENT AT ROANOKE

As soon as John White was back in England in November of 1587, he rushed to Raleigh with news of the colony's situation and threw himself into preparations for his return with supplies and new settlers. Raleigh was equally enthusiastic and decided to send a small ship, a pinnace, right away with immediate necessities and with news that a major supply fleet would follow, "God willing," the next summer. In fact, the colonists were never to be seen again by any European; they were lost from this time forward. All ventures were risky in the extreme, because the margin between success and failure was paper thin. In the case of the final Roanoke colony, all the chances went against rather than for them.

The pinnace never sailed, possibly because departure of the main convoy was scheduled so early that it was thought unnecessary, or because winter weather made the voyage too risky. Raleigh set about preparing a supply fleet of seven or eight ships to sail early in the spring of 1588 under Sir Richard Grenville. Supplies, ships, and men were assembled at Bideford in the West of England. Raleigh also arranged for the publication of Thomas Hariot's *Brief and True Report of the New Found Land of Virginia* to attract investors. Just as the fleet was ready, an order arrived forbidding it to sail. In fact the Privy Council forbade any ships capable of service in war to leave English harbors. The King of Spain's great Armada, whose goal was to crush England's naval power and pave the way for an invasion, was rumored to be ready to sail, and Elizabeth wanted to take no chances with the country's defense. Once again, and in the most fateful way, the connection between privateering and colonization ruined Roanoke's chances of success.

Spain had been able to accept some degree of preying on its treasure fleet, but since the all-out sea war had begun in 1585, the level had become intolerable. The treasure of the Indies, once a luxury, had enabled Spain to build the most elaborate centralized machinery of government for its far-flung possessions of any state in Europe. Running this cumbersome bureaucracy and the war machine that supported it was extravagantly expensive; the yearly influx of gold and silver from America was now an absolute necessity. It was galling that it should be little England, the leader of the Protestant nations, that caused Philip II, supporter of the most rigid Catholicism, such difficulties. Philip decided to cut off the problem at its source by crippling, possibly even conquering, England. The fleet he assembled to accomplish his purpose, one hundred and thirty ships with eight thousand sailors and nineteen thousand soldiers, was the most impressive in history. Elizabeth was right to be afraid.[1]

England's greatness at sea began with the defeat of the Armada. When the two fleets met, the greater maneuverability of the English ships gave the victory to the underdog, but that was no accident. Veterans of West Indian raids on Spanish possessions, led by Sir John Hawkins, the treasurer of the queen's navy, had revolutionized the basic concepts of war at sea. The major ships of the British navy had been rebuilt to accommodate this conceptual shift. Formerly, ships were seen as floating battlefields, whose only purpose was to transport soldiers and bring them close enough to board enemy ships and fight as they would on land. Everything in ship design had been subordinated to the needs of the soldiers; there were high wooden castles fore and aft to provide shelter in battle, making the ships very clumsy sailers.

Hawkins, seconded by Drake, realized that ships should be the principal weapons at sea. They redesigned the fleet, removing the bulky castles and making the ships much more maneuverable. The English fleet, riding lower in the water and equipped with longer-range guns, sought to cripple the enemy's ships from a distance. The changes made sailing skill of prime importance; no longer was the sailor to take a back seat to the soldier at sea. The English fleet was better equipped and more flexible than the old-fashioned Spanish fleet when they met in the English Channel in the summer of 1588. Raleigh was involved in the development of the new design. His *Ark Raleigh* was considered one of the best; when he gave it to the queen, it was renamed the *Ark*

Royal and became the flagship of the English navy. Raleigh's ship carried Lord Admiral Charles Howard when the fleet confronted the
Armada.

Drake's boldness may have affected Philip II's plans, and therefore
the colony's fate, in another way: the great Spanish fleet had been ready
to sail in 1587 when Drake attacked Cadiz and wreaked such havoc that
its departure was delayed. If the Armada had sailed in 1587 as planned,
White's colony would not have embarked then, and its history would
have been quite different.

There were other ways in which the Armada robbed the Roanoke
colony of its future. For a time, the attention of all the country's
leaders was focused on it. Ralph Lane, Raleigh, and Grenville were
appointed to a committee to plan the overall defense of the realm,
which reported its findings in November 1587, the same month White
returned from America. Raleigh and Grenville were given the job of
organizing the defense of England's West Country should the Spaniards, possibly attempting to capitalize on Irish disaffection, attempt an
invasion there. Neither man had much time or attention to spare for
American colonies. Even after the depleted Armada disappeared
around the northern tip of the British Isles where, though the English
did not know it, about half the fleet was broken up by storms on the
rocky coastline, Grenville and Raleigh's vigilance continued through
the autumn and into the winter because the perceived danger to
England's West continued. Since no one knew for sure of the Armada's
plight, they stood ready to ferry troops to Ireland if invasion
threatened from there.

Moreover, both men had acquired vast new plantations in Ireland.
The English government's strategy for pacifying Ireland was to make
large land grants, the confiscated property of defeated rebels, to groups
of "undertakers," so called because they undertook to settle English
families, headed by farmers and other skilled persons, on the land,
thereby recreating their own society. The queen made it clear that
such colonization must be carried out or the grants would be with-
drawn. The government's attitude toward Irish colonies, where the
nation's safety was seen to be involved, was everything American
promoters could have wished. There was a massive propaganda campaign to attract settlers and investors, and the full weight of the crown
was put behind the effort.

Raleigh and Grenville were two of the greatest beneficiaries of the land bonanza, and Raleigh devoted much of his attention during 1587 and 1588 to signing up and ferrying over colonists. By the time he himself went to inspect in the fall of 1589, he had several hundred planters on his Irish properties. In comparison to the Armada campaign and the excitement over Irish plantations, Roanoke must have seemed very small and far away. Precisely what the colonists feared was in fact happening: America was slipping to the bottom of the long list of enterprises that Raleigh and his associates were interested in.

White alone had continued to work exclusively for his colonists. While England awaited the Armada, he managed to get permission to detach two of the smaller ships from Grenville's fleet and take them with a few new colonists and some supplies so that the settlers at Roanoke would know they had not been deserted. The *Brave* of thirty tons and the *Roe,* twenty-five tons, sailed on April 22nd, 1588 with fifteen planters, men and women, the latter perhaps wives of men already in America, and supplies. John White knew that spring, when the food supply was consumed and crops were not yet ready, was the most difficult time of year in a new colony, and that the settlers already in America would not be able to call on Indian help as Lane's men had done.

The anguish and frustration White experienced on this voyage can still be felt in every line of his narrative. Once again the conception of Roanoke as a mere adjunct to privateering haunted the colony because, to the sailors, piracy was the primary goal of their voyage. England needed its best men as well as ships to confront the Armada, so the men Grenville allowed to go with White were very probably the dregs of the assembled fleet. Only one day out of England, they began indiscriminately attacking ships, including one from Scotland and a Breton from France. White's purpose was doomed. His journal was punctuated by accounts of almost daily pursuits, with these tiny vessels taking on ships as big as two hundred tons. The *Brave* was most active in all this; the *Roe* was a very clumsy sailer, possibly because it was overloaded. By May 3rd the two ships had become separated, and the *Brave* sailed on toward Madeira.

There the tables were turned on the privateers: they had a nominally friendly encounter with a ship from La Rochelle, but the French ship was just scouting in preparation for later attack. It and its consort,

having taken the measure of the *Brave,* attacked the next day; the battle raged for one and one-half hours in hand-to-hand combat on both
ships. Many men were killed or injured, and the English lost their
food, powder, and weapons, and all the supplies intended for the
colonists. The master and mate of White's ship were critically
wounded, and the master gunner was dead. White himself said that he
was wounded twice in the head, "once with a sword, and another time
with a pike, and hurt also in the side of the buttock with a shot."
Three of the intended colonists were injured, one in ten or twelve
places. After the English powder ran out, the French overwhelmed
their ship; and White thought all the passengers and sailors of the
Brave were to be put to death in retaliation for the great number of
dead and injured in the French ship. The fury of the sailors was
controlled with difficulty by the French captain; it was turned instead
to carrying away everything they could from the *Brave,* which they continued all the next day. So greedy were the French sailors that they
overloaded and split the small boats belonging to both their ship and
the *Brave.* This was fortunate, because they were forced to quit looting
while the English still had their sails and two anchors.

The intention of sailing to America now had to be given up, and all
able hands fell to repairing the rigging and mending the sails so they
could make their way home to England as best they could. Not only
had they lost the services of their chief officers, but the French had also
taken their pilot, Pedro Díaz, who had been captured with his ship by
Grenville in 1585 and was serving unwillingly. The English feared
they could not navigate without him. They kept their course as far
west as they could, because they could not afford to risk meeting
another warship. The *Brave* arrived back at Bideford exactly one
month after it had left. The *Roe* came back a few weeks later, also
without having gone to Virginia. White believed that the "cruel
fight" his ship had endured was just punishment by God for the
"thievery of our evil disposed mariners," but its effects fell most
heavily on the innocent colonists at Roanoke.

White continued to fight for his colonists; as Raleigh's interest was
waning, he sought other investors. In March 1589, a new corporation
was set up to support the colony assumed to be still in existence in
America; in form, it was an agreement between Raleigh on one side

and a group of powerful merchants and colonial promoters on the other. Hariot's book on the resources of Roanoke must have been crucial in attracting the merchants, who would not invest unless there was a good chance of return. Their presence in the syndicate was very important because they had the economic resources to keep the colony going. In addition to the merchants, the corporation included the younger Richard Hakluyt; a mathematician named Thomas Hoode, whose work was important in the development of navigational theory; and John Gerard, who wrote a widely used herbal, an encyclopedic listing of plants from all over the world with descriptions of their medicinal and culinary properties. The group also included most of the original assistants and a new man recruited by White. Simon Fernandes was not mentioned. The syndicate agreed to contribute money and supplies as well as the ships to send them to the colony; in return, Raleigh guaranteed them and their heirs free trade with all his American lands for seven years. Raleigh also made a free gift of £100 to the enterprise. The new corporation confirmed the colony's administration by a governor and twelve assistants as set up by the 1587 agreement. Raleigh promised that he would try to get letters patent from the queen to confirm the contract and ensure that it was legally binding.

Though there is evidence that at least some of these merchants did invest considerable sums in attempts to reach the colony in 1590 and after, no ship was sent in 1589. Since the agreement was signed in March, this failure is hard to understand. Presumably, the syndicate was amassing the necessary funds during the early summer and then found that it was too late in the year to send a fleet. Nothing exists to indicate John White's feelings as the year passed. His anxiety must have been assuaged as 1590 brought a great deal of activity, including his last voyage to America in search of his colony.

White was more eager than the merchants to embark for Roanoke. Early in 1590 he learned of two facts that he thought he could use to the colony's advantage. The great merchant and privateering investor, John Watts, had prepared three ships, the *Hopewell,* the *John Evangelist,* and the *Little John,* for West Indian adventuring; but just as they were ready to sail, another general stay of shipping was issued by the Privy Council, which feared a renewed Spanish attack. White had the idea that if he could tell the authorities Watts' ships would carry settlers and supplies to Roanoke, then they might be released from the ban, which would please both Watts and the corporation.

One of the merchants in the syndicate, William Sanderson, was also preparing a ship, the *Moonlight*, with supplies for the colony. It was expected that Sanderson's ship would become a consort of Watts' three. Watts was supposed to give Raleigh a bond of £3000 for performance of this contract, but White said that it was never paid. Nor did Watts live up to his bargain. When the time for departure came, his commanders told White that they would take nothing but him and his sea chest, "no not so much as a boy to attend upon me." White said he protested this "cross and unkind dealing" to the ships' masters and to Watts himself; but, since there was not time to inform Raleigh, he accepted the terms rather than lose the chance of going altogether. The *Moonlight* was also left behind, but embarked later.

Governor White was playing a dangerous game in making use of the association of privateering with colonization that he abhorred, and he lived to regret it bitterly. The *Hopewell, John Evangelist,* and *Little John* made straight for the West Indies and the rich prizes they hoped to capture. Near the Canaries, they made their first capture, a ship loaded with wine and cinnamon. It was sent back to England manned by a prize crew from the English ships. In the West Indies, the *Hopewell* and the *John Evangelist* separated from the *Little John,* which stayed off Dominica looking for the treasure fleet. The others captured a boat loaded with ginger and hides near Puerto Rico, but they suffered a loss there: their pilot, a mulatto named Pedro "who knew all our state" ran away to the Spaniards. Pedro was able to tell the Spanish much about the English and their plans, a vivid reminder of how vulnerable their lack of navigational skills made the English. As long as they were forced to rely on captive foreigners for pilots, they ran the risk of all kinds of treachery.

After the ships left Puerto Rico, they landed on the small island of Mona, where they burned a Spanish village of ten or twelve houses and took a pinnace; the inhabitants fled to the woods and caves and could not be found. In a few days, they again met the *Little John,* and the three ships stationed themselves at either end of Hispaniola, hoping to catch sight of the Spanish treasure fleet. White included a small incident that conveys a different impression of life at sea than the constant recitation of sea fights. One of the boys with the English ran away at Cape Tiburon, Hispaniola, and returned ten days later, starving. White said that the region was littered with the bones of men

who had starved; he thought they either had been shipwrecked or were
stragglers from warships. One would like to know more about what
the boy was running from or to, and how he was treated on his return.

White's frustration was growing daily. He told Richard Hakluyt in
a private letter that he went to the ship's master with "daily and con-
tinual petitions" that they move on to the aid of the colony in
accordance with their promise to Raleigh. It is hard not to believe that
White was his own worst enemy; in all his dealings as governor, he
showed an inability to command effectively or to get people to see
things his way. Perhaps control of the situation when privateering was
at stake was more than anyone could accomplish. In any case, his complaining must have hardened attitudes against him and the colony
among the crew he daily harangued.

Weeks went by and more ships were approached; some were disap-
pointments, some were better. Once, they captured a ship with just
three men in it, fugitives escaped from prison who were going to join a
colony of buccaneers in western Hispaniola. One of these was an
experienced pilot who joined the English, making up the gap in experience left by Pedro's desertion. The *Moonlight*, Sanderson's ship that
had been left behind in England, arrived early in July. It was accompanied by a pinnace, the *Conclude*, that had been invited to sail as its
consort only until the *Moonlight* came up to Watts's ships. The same
day, the crews sighted a fleet of fourteen ships from Santo Domingo.
As the Spanish fleet scattered, so did the English ships; the *Moonlight*,
its temporary consort, and the *Hopewell* together happened to corner
the vice-admiral of the Spanish fleet, the *Buen Jesús*. It proved to be a
rich prize and the subject of a heated court fight later over the division
of spoils, because the consortship status of the three vessels had not
been determined in advance.

For the rest of the month of July, the scattered fleet cruised in the
West Indies. They found themselves so "pestered" with the Spaniards
they had accumulated with the captured ships that these were dropped
off on various islands. Finally, at the beginning of August, the *Buen
Jesús* was sent to England, and the *Hopewell* and the *Moonlight* moved
out to catch the strong coastal current that would help propel them to
Virginia. They had waited for the *Little John* and the *John Evangelist* to
no avail. The latter two ships had had a disappointing time; they had
fought with and captured several rich prizes only to see them sink

before they could be unloaded, so fierce had the fighting been. One of the lost cargoes included thirteen pipes, or large crates, of silver. Finally, they had gone to join the English ships waiting off the Azores in hopes of catching the Spanish treasure fleet.

John White's excitement at finally being set for Roanoke met further checks; there were continuous storms during the first ten days of August. Then the ships began to move along the Outer Banks, taking on water near the modern Cape Lookout. Finally, in mid-August they anchored offshore, near enough to see Roanoke. White was gratified to see smoke rising from the area where he had left the colony, but it was evening and they decided to wait till morning to go ashore. Two boats full of men embarked then; seeing smoke from another place, on Hatarask Island, they decided to go there first. After a long, hot march without any fresh water, they were disappointed to find no sign of human beings, the fire having been naturally kindled. They decided to wait until the next day to go to Roanoke Island, meanwhile filling casks with fresh water found by digging in the sand dunes.

Next morning they got a slow start as they again sought water in the dunes, and they finally set off about ten o'clock in such high waves that all the powder, shot, and food in the first boat was ruined. The second boat was completely overturned in trying to cross through the treacherous inlet; seven of the men, including Captain Edward Spicer of the *Moonlight,* Ralph Skinner, his mate, and "Hance the surgeon," were drowned. So upset were the sailors that they refused to go any further in search of the colonists; only the firmness of White and of Captain Abraham Cocke of the *Hopewell* persuaded them to go on.

By the time they reached the area of the colony, it was dark, so they anchored their boats to wait for daylight. They could see a great fire burning through the trees. Once they were actually that close, Governor White must have been able to communicate some of the excitement he felt at seeing the fire, for the sailors participated with him in an all-night songfest. To reassure the colonists that they were a friendly party, they first sounded a trumpet and then spent the night singing English folk tunes and calling out familiar greetings, but no answer came. At dawn, they went first to the area of the fire and found that it was just grass and rotted trees burning, probably kindled by natural causes. They then took a roundabout route to the north end of the island, where the village had been when White left the settlers.

During this march, they found the footprints of two or three Indians. Their movements were being observed.

Near the village, the party found a tree with CRO carved on it in "fair Roman letters." This was the secret sign White and the colonists had agreed upon before his departure. Before White left them, the colonists had discussed leaving Roanoke Island and moving up into the interior, fulfilling the plans for the City of Raleigh; so White was not alarmed to find them gone. He revealed that he and the planters had agreed they would carve on trees or doorposts the name of the place where they had moved so that, when he came with supplies, he would be able to find them. Further, they were to carve a Maltese cross over the name if they left in distress, and there was no cross!

As they approached the village site, White saw that all the houses had been dismantled, possibly so that at least some parts of them could be transported to the settlers' new home. A strong palisade had been erected around the site where the houses had been. On one of the entrance posts was carved CROATOAN, again without any distress signal. Inside the enclosure, they found scattered about several of the large guns left with the colonists and some bars of iron and pigs of lead, which would have been too heavy to carry; but all the smaller ordnance was gone. There were other signs that the colonists had made an orderly departure: some sailors independently found they had buried chests in a trench, which the Indians had later dug up and left to spoil. This was the colonists' attempt to make good on their promise to White to safeguard his possessions, but everything was ruined. White's lament allows us to see the life he had originally envisioned in the wilderness. He wrote of "my books torn from the covers, the frames of some of my pictures and Maps rotten and spoiled with rain, and my armor almost eaten through with rust." White considered that the colonists had kept their promise, however; and he was glad that they were safe at Croatoan, "which is the place where Manteo was born, and the Savages of the Island our friends."

The men hurried to their boats after surveying the colony site because they wanted to be on board ship before nightfall. There were signs that a "foul and stormy night" was brewing; in fact the weather was so bad that they feared losing their anchor and cable. Next morning, they decided to move the ships down toward Croatoan. As they were completing the winding of the anchor cable around the capstan, the cable broke, and they lost that anchor and then another in their efforts to avoid being driven onshore and wrecked. As a result, only one of the original four anchors was left on the *Hopewell,* and their supply of food was running low. Moreover, they had abandoned their cask of fresh water on Roanoke the evening before when the threatening storm had driven them to their ships. They decided to go back to the West Indies to obtain food and water and then to winter there, with the intention of returning to Croatoan in the spring. White was delighted with the plan; the only problem was convincing the new master of the *Moonlight.* He begged off on the grounds that his "weak and leak ship" was not able to continue. Therefore, the *Moonlight* set off for England, and the *Hopewell* made its way toward Trinidad.

Once again foul weather changed their plans for them. A great storm blew the *Hopewell* out to sea. Now the master had a difficult decision to make: should he still attempt to go the West Indies, or should he go on to the Azores where he knew there was a large gathering of English ships waiting for the Spanish treasure fleet? This was a particularly difficult decision because sixteenth-century sailors had no way of determining their longitude. Latitude could be judged with fairly great accuracy by using the astrolabe or cross-staff, which measured the elevation of the sun above the horizon at noon, though its precision could be greatly affected by the movement of the ship's deck. In judging how far east or west they had traveled, it was a matter of dead reckoning, guessing speed in relation to time elapsed. Storms threw out such calculations and made determination of location very difficult.

The master of the *Hopewell* decided that they were so far east they should make for the Azores. They hoped not only to take on fresh water, but to obtain food and other supplies from some of the English men-of-war before returning to the West Indies. They arrived about the middle of September, after experiencing many contrary winds, and confronted a ship that happened to be a prize taken in the West Indies by their consort ship, the *Little John.* From its men, they learned of the problems that had beset the *Little John* and *John Evangelist.* In Flores harbor, they met many English ships, including the *Mary Rose,* flagship of the queen's fleet, "wherein was General Sir John Hawkins," and the supposedly crippled *Moonlight,* whose crew shamefacedly set sail for England as soon as they spotted the *Hopewell.*

Hawkins decided to leave the Azores and spread the fleet along the coasts of Spain and Portugal, but no treasure ships were captured. Spain was learning how to cope with the privateers; the gold and silver of America were now increasingly being shipped in the new fast *galizabras* that slipped through the English fleet unlike the old clumsy convoys. Part of the treasure fleet had already reached Spain; the rest had been held back at Havana till the next year. There was nothing for the English to catch by this time. The *Hopewell* remained with the fleet about a week and then made for England, not for the West Indies as planned. They may have had less luck in obtaining supplies in the Azores than they had anticipated, or there may have been pressure from the men who wanted to be in England when the riches of the *Buen Jesús* were divided up. Whatever the reason, White had made his last attempt to reach the lost colonists.

John White wrote narratives of all his voyages at the urging of Richard Hakluyt, who published them in his great compilation, *The Principal Navigations, Voyages, Traffics, and Discoveries of the English Nation.* This last narrative was sent in 1593 from White's new home at Newtown in County Cork, Ireland, where he was again one of Raleigh's colonists. Though he continued to worry and agitate about the fate of the Roanoke colony, he had begun a new life. He enclosed with the narrative a letter to Hakluyt in which his pain was eloquently expressed. In it, he indicated he had spent his own money in his search for the colony and said that he "would to God my wealth were answerable to my will." At the end he committed the colonists to God's care and prayed they would be helped and comforted.

Though 1590 saw White's last failure as a colonial promoter, he also had a considerable achievement in that year, one that has been very important ever since. That was the year that Theodore DeBry of Frankfurt began publishing his definitive compilation of accounts of all American voyages. Thomas Hariot's *Brief and True Report of the Newfound Land of Virginia* was reprinted in volume I of *America*, accompanied by the DeBry engravings of White's watercolors with Hariot's notes. The woodcuts were not completely faithful to White's originals, and therefore some of his ethnographic accuracy was lost; but they were the best portrayals of American Indians available for centuries, and they were reproduced many times to illustrate studies of Indians far removed from Roanoke. White began his association with

America as a painter and it was his art that has been his greatest contribution to history, one that is more fully appreciated in modern times as his original watercolors have been displayed and published. The record he left of the Indians on the shores of North Carolina is considered the best done anywhere in America before the advent of photography. Because of the White-Hariot collaboration, English chronicling of the American Indians began at its highest point, a level not reached again for centuries.

For ten years, nothing much was done about looking for the colonists. Raleigh was involved in multitudes of other projects and had lost much of his personal power. Moreover, as long as he could claim that the colonists still lived, his patent, which required him to have a settlement in existence, was protected. There may have come a point when he no longer wanted to search for the colonists because he did not want to risk producing proof that they were dead and his colony truly lost. John Gerard, syndicate member, wrote somewhat gloomily in his 1597 *Herbal* that the planters were still alive if "murdering, or pestilence, corrupt air, bloody fluxes [dysentery], or some other mortal sickness hath not destroyed them." In this way, the colony was kept before the public mind. There are some vague hints that privateering voyages from time to time coasted along the Outer Banks on their way home from the West Indies, but none reported seeing the colonists.

Finally in the beginning of the new century, Raleigh's interest in his American colonies reawakened and he began to send out voyages again. A brief note about a voyage of Samuel Mace, "a very sufficient Mariner, an honest sober man" was printed in 1602, which claimed that Mace had been to Virginia twice before. The note asserted that Raleigh had been disgusted at the antics and dereliction of duty of the earlier voyages such as those White had sailed on, so he bought his own ship and "hired all the company for wages by the month." This last telling phrase indicates what was wrong all those times before. The voyages had been financed by privateering, which meant that the sailors' income was entirely from the spoils taken. In those circumstances, it is small wonder that they put privateering first.

Raleigh's gesture of actually hiring a crew and paying them came too late: this expedition also failed to make a search for the lost colony. This may have been due at least partly to Raleigh's desire to make some money from the voyage. The ship first landed on the Outer

Banks some distance south of the inlet to Roanoke and spent about a month cutting and loading wood and roots in demand in Europe for their scent or supposed medicinal value. Sassafras was one such plant; its importation brought enormous monetary returns before the market became flooded early in the seventeenth century.

When the mariners finally turned their attention to the problem of the settlement, they said that the weather was then too stormy and they had lost some of their tackle, so they turned back without finding the colonists. Financing expeditions to America purely through private enterprise brought insurmountable problems unless massive backing could be arranged. The overwhelming need to have each venture pay its own way tended to swamp all other considerations. Raleigh may have been planning further voyages when fate intervened: Queen Elizabeth died in 1603. The new king, James I, believed Raleigh was a traitor and soon placed him under arrest in the Tower of London.

Raleigh and White were not the only ones looking for the colony. The Spanish had heard all kinds of reports, some very far from the truth, and wanted to find Roanoke to extinguish it. Spain claimed North America at least as far north as Chesapeake Bay, their Bahía de Santa María de Jacán. The Spanish had earlier made good on their claims when they had extinguished French Huguenot colonies in Florida and South Carolina and founded a Jesuit mission on the York River in modern Virginia in 1570. Moreover, Spanish authorities knew that the primary purpose of Raleigh's colony was to serve as a privateering base, so they were not disposed to let it remain.

Their major problem was gathering accurate information about Roanoke; most of what they had came from renegades, usually men like the two Pedros who had been forced to work for the English for a time, from Spanish colonists who had been visited by English vessels, or from the crews of ships that had been seized by privateers. Such information was often wildly inaccurate, frequently in the direction of making the colony sound larger or more successful than it really was; so the Spanish colonial governors lived in a state of quite unnecessary alarm about what the English were doing. Early reports had indicated that Grenville, called Campo Verde in Spanish dispatches, had left as many as five hundred men and five ships in America in 1585, and that he was returning immediately from England with further supplies. In 1590,

Puerto Rico authorities were told by survivors of the *Buen Jesús* that forty English vessels had been sent to Roanoke and that, in the next year, one hundred and fifty were coming to prey on the Indies. When men such as Pedro Díaz accurately portrayed the small scale and weak situation of the colony, the governors did not know whom to trust.

A Spanish expedition found traces of the colony, but only by accident, partly because they always looked in the wrong place. They knew that the Outer Banks were inadequate for a privateering base, so they assumed the English could not have deposited colonists there. They combed Chesapeake Bay looking for the colony, and even after their find on the Outer Banks, they continued to assume the main settlement was to the north. Several times plans were made to eliminate altogether the worry caused by an English settlement so nearby. When the effect of Drake's devastating year of raiding in 1585–1586 was combined with news that Lane had established the first Roanoke colony, the Spanish governor of Florida developed plans to acquire a fleet of four ships from Spain, extinguish the Roanoke colony, and then establish a fortress of three hundred soldiers on Chesapeake Bay to forestall future English adventuring there. The immediate requirement of protecting the treasure fleet came first, however, and that voyage never took place. So pressing was the need to cope with the threat an English colony posed, though, that in 1588 King Philip seriously considered diverting part of the great Armada to attack the English in America.

The sea war with England prevented Spain from moving effectively against the colony just as it kept Raleigh from supplying Roanoke; ironically, Spanish concern about the colony was at its height after the English had virtually given up the idea of a base. In 1600, the newly appointed governor of Spanish Florida called for an expedition to destroy the settlers on Chesapeake Bay. He had discovered Darby Glavin among his soldiers and had heard a very interesting story from him. Glavin was the Irish renegade who had been in the Lane colony and then had deserted on Puerto Rico from White's group rather than return to Roanoke. He had been condemned to the Spanish galleys for many years, but had finally been released and allowed to join the Spanish army. The governor pumped him for news of Roanoke.

Glavin was only too happy to tell all about the difficulties of Lane's colony, and added the information that the settlers had found gold and pearls there, which made it seem unlikely to the Florida governor that Raleigh would have abandoned the area. Glavin asserted that the White colonists were still alive and were on Chesapeake Bay, where he assumed they had gone from the beginning. His account seemed credible because he claimed to have talked to some English survivors of an ill-fated 1593 Pacific expedition led by Richard Hawkins, who told him they had been joined for a time after leaving England by two ships loaded with supplies and settlers for Roanoke. No other record of such ships exists. On the strength of Glavin's information, the governor asked for an army of a thousand soldiers to move against the English on Chesapeake Bay. His request was ignored at home. In fact, by 1600 Spain was considering pulling back from its commitments in North America and consolidating the empire. Thus, one possible clue to the fate of the colonists is a dead end: Spain would have eliminated them, but was unable to do so.

Where were the colonists? Though they were never seen again by Europeans, some hints were gleaned about their ultimate fate. When Jamestown, the first successful English colony, was founded on Chesapeake Bay in 1607, twenty years after the abandonment of the Roanoke colonists, the settlers heard some tantalizing stories about people like them living with Indians there. The Virginia Company made the search for such colonists a top priority, because they knew that if the Jamestown settlers could draw on their twenty years' experience of the country, the new colony would have an infinitely easier time getting established. Moreover, there would have to be no slow and painstaking search for the country's wealth, and the investors in England could begin to reap rewards instantly. Captain John Smith published a book about Virginia and his exploits there in 1608, the year after the colony was founded; he reported that Indians had told him of people like the settlers, whom Smith took to be the lost colonists. Another colonist, George Percy, reported that he had seen a young Indian boy of about ten whose hair was "a perfect yellow" and with a "reasonable white skin, which is a Miracle amongst all Savages." During his presidency Smith sent two missions to the south, looking for evidence that the Roanoke colonists were alive and hoping to establish communication with them. The Virginia settlers were hopeful during the first year or so; but, about the end of 1608, they learned that the earlier colonists had been killed.

In 1612, William Strachey, a gentleman of literary pretensions who had gone to Virginia to be the secretary of the Jamestown colony, wrote his *History of Travel into Virginia Britannia*. He reported that the Roanoke colonists had made their way from the Outer Banks to Chesapeake Bay, thus fulfilling the original plan for the colony. They had lived in peace for twenty years with Indians outside the domain of the "Great Emperor" Powhatan, in whose territory Jamestown had been founded.[2] Urged on by his priests, who prophesied that a rival to him would emerge from the Chesapeakes, the tribe sheltering the Roanoke refugees, Powhatan ordered the slaughter of them all, English and Indians. Ironically, this had happened just at the time the Virginia colonists were first arriving. Strachey claimed that four men, two boys, and a young girl had escaped and were living to the south with Indians who had stone houses of more than one story, a style taught them by the English. He indicated that these survivors were valued because they knew how to work copper.

Often the reports heard by the colonists came from Indians who may have had their own reasons, such as enmity toward Powhatan, to pass them on; some may have been saying what they thought the colonists wanted to hear. There certainly are false or fanciful elements in most of them. Kemps, or Machumps, the informer Strachey quoted about the surviving seven colonists, went on to say that the Indians with whom they lived kept tame turkeys and "take Apes in the Mountains." He was a captive whom John Smith originally described as one of "the two most exact villains in the country." Kemps apparently came to love and respect the colonists and aided them both before and after his release, but his case illustrates the difficulty of obtaining accurate information. There was, much later, corroboration of this story, however. Though Smith never mentioned it in his own writings, his friend, Samuel Purchas, who continued the Hakluyt tradition of editing and publishing chronicles of English voyages, said in 1625 that Powhatan himself had confessed to Smith his part in the settlers' killings and had shown him "divers utensils of theirs."

Such a report, though not so complete, had apparently been circulating in the Virginia Company in England for some time when Strachey first wrote the full story in 1612. The *Instructions* sent to the governor in Virginia in 1609 mentioned the slaughter, as did a promotional pamphlet published in England in 1610. Both, though, found hope in the idea that some of the colonists had escaped. The 1609 *Instructions* ordered the governor to find the four colonists then believed to be still alive. The *True and Sincere Declaration of the Purpose of the Plantation begun in Virginia* claimed that two explorers from Jamestown had actually seen evidence of the Roanoke planters in the form of newly carved crosses and letters on trees. They believed the Indians had deliberately kept them from talking to their compatriots, but that the company lived about fifty miles from Jamestown and could easily be contacted, after which they could "open the womb and bowels of this country" to the newcomers. No one explained, then or later, why nothing was done to find and talk to these English people who were thought to be living so close by.

How can reports that the Roanoke colonists made their way to Chesapeake Bay be reconciled with the evidence White found that they had in fact gone south to Croatoan Island? Professor David Quinn proposes that both indications may be true. Probably the bulk of the colonists did go up to Chesapeake Bay and lived there in peace among the Indians for twenty years; in fact they may have left shortly after White and the ships departed. Since no precise destination for the colony's move had been agreed on before White left, the colonists would have left a holding party behind to guide the supply ships when they came, to protect the heavy equipment that could not be moved, and to maintain the settlement in case Raleigh wanted to develop it as a base in the future. The need for protection of such a small group would account for the palisade around the dismantled village. At some point, then, the holding party may have found their situation untenable, possibly because of Indian hostility, and may have decided to move south to the protection of Manteo and the friendly Croatoans. These people would have left the CROATOAN carvings on the tree and post at Roanoke. Thus, when White came to Roanoke in 1590, some of his colonists may actually have been quite close by on the Outer Banks, even if most were on Chesapeake Bay.[3]

The story of the lost colony at Roanoke is one of lost chances and near misses, some agonizingly close. If any one of a number of ventures had been conducted differently, if weather patterns had changed slightly, the colony might not have been abandoned. One lesson that promoters learned from this failed venture was that a successful colony could not be planned on such a small scale. Much greater and more consistent backing would be required to found an American colony capable of succeeding. Roanoke's near misses happened partly because the entire venture rested on a handful of men who were either too insignificant to carry it on, or were involved in too many other schemes to focus sufficiently clearly on this one enterprise. When the next colony, Jamestown, was planned, a large company of investors was assembled, and men with money to spend and those with the essential connections at court were part of the company. The Virginia Company learned a great deal from the mistakes of Roanoke, though some of those mistakes were nonetheless repeated.

9

ENDINGS

LOCAL legends in North Carolina maintain that the lost colonists survived and intermarried with the Indians and that their descendants live in the region today. The Lumbee Indians of Robeson County, North Carolina, believe they are those descendants.[1] It is certainly possible that some of the Roanoke colonists did live on and melt into the native population. This could have been true of the several hundred slaves and Indians from the Caribbean left by Drake, the three men abandoned by Lane's colony in their haste to leave, or the fifteen men left by Grenville when he found the colony deserted in 1586, as well as of the men, women, and children left by John White in 1587. If William Strachey's report of children being saved from Powhatan's vengeance is correct, then a completely American generation had begun to grow up; Virginia Dare, if she was alive, would have been a young woman when English colonists again came to Virginia, possibly a mother herself.

If some of the colonists returned to or stayed in North Carolina, though, they would have shared the disasters that came upon the region's Indians throughout the colonial period. The colony of Carolina, later separated into North and South Carolina, was founded in the late seventeenth century. Contemporary reports speak of great mortality, probably from disease, among the Indians at that time, and many of the Carolina Algonquians were killed during the war between the colony and the Tuscarora Indians in the early eighteenth century. By the end of the colonial period there were only a few left, and they had lost most of their lands. Though they continued their precontact subsistence patterns and kept up native crafts, the Indians were infiltrated by European habits and demoralized by alcholic beverages. It is impossible in the twentieth century to recognize remnants of the tribes described in the early documents. They live on in White's paintings and Hariot's commentary, but the proud, strong people portrayed there were ultimately both vanquished and seduced by European culture.

The Outer Banks were resettled, largely from Virginia, with the founding of the Carolina colony in the 1660s. The islands were valuable for stock raising, supplemented by fishing and some small-scale agriculture. There was also an echo of its earlier life: at the end of the seventeenth century and the beginning of the eighteenth, the entire coastal region was used by pirates and smugglers. The honeycomb of small coves and hidden inlets suited these pirates, who included Captain Teach, the famous Blackbeard. Once the pirates were eliminated, fishing became the major source of income among the sparse population of the Outer Banks. Now tourism holds that position. Though the Outer Banks never prospered as colonial promoters had hoped, the later Carolina colony, particularly South Carolina, did produce lavish returns through rice and indigo production and became the richest of the English colonies on the American mainland.

England forgot its interest in American settlements for twenty years after the lost colonists were left at Roanoke. Some of the most important people backing plantations had died; the elder Richard Hakluyt died in 1591, and Secretary Walsingham, the most influential person who encouraged such ventures, in 1589. No one of equal stature took over Walsingham's role. 1588 was a crucial turning point after which England could have made a bid to become a major power in the Atlantic, but that would not happen without the open and consistent support of Queen Elizabeth, and the man who could have convinced her of the need for such investment was gone. Interest in the Atlantic did not die, but dissolved into a welter of private goals and ventures. The merchants saw Roanoke as an expensive failure; all the income they had gleaned from connection with it had been from privateering, and the colony had contributed nothing to that. Moreover, some of the hoped-for benefits of a colony were being realized without it; English ships were beginning to stay longer in the Caribbean. Therefore, the money and energy of English promoters went into privateering for the next decade.

The 1590s were the great period of privateering in the Elizabethan sea war with Spain, on a scale much larger than that of the 1580s. Raleigh was heavily involved in such ventures; in 1591, he joined with

John Watts, forgetting the latter's treachery of the previous year, in a tremendously profitable voyage. Such successes fed the desire of Raleigh and others to invest even more in subsequent expeditions. During this decade, privateering ventures brought in cargoes worth from £ 100,000 to £ 300,000 each year, which amounted to between 10 and 15 percent of England's total imports. Merchants were increasingly involved, with their ships often combining legitimate trade and plundering. Such activities did not mean loss of dignity or status: John Watts, the greatest promoter of privateering, had become, by the beginning of the seventeenth century, the leading merchant of London. The motivation of the privateers was correctly seen as a mixture of patriotism and profit.

Grenville was a casualty of this sea war. The manner of his death, in a fight off the Azores, made him one of the great Elizabethan heroes. In 1591 the English resumed the previous year's strategy in attempting to snare the treasure fleet, a prospect especially attractive because they knew a double load of treasure would be on it. A large flotilla was to stay off the Azores with small fast pinnaces stationed along the route to bring news of the Spanish fleet's departure and progress. The English arrived early and had a long wait. By the end of the summer the English ships were in need of rummaging and cleaning after four months at sea. This was somewhat risky because they knew the treasure fleet must have left Havana some time before, but they stationed a pinnace to the west to inform them of any sightings. What the commander, Lord Thomas Howard, did not know was that a battle formation was approaching from the east with the intention of destroying the English.

King Philip of Spain had turned his attention to renewing his fleet immediately after the disaster of the Armada and had built twelve great new ships, named after the twelve apostles, on the English model. Though the English thought of the Spanish navy as still crippled, it was in fact prepared to fight again. The surprised English managed to scurry away from the threat, except for Grenville, vice admiral of the fleet, in the *Revenge*. Most of his men were still on shore when the enemy appeared. The English ships attempted to circle around and get to windward of the Spanish to draw them away from the *Revenge*. Grenville could have simply sailed away and escaped; but this was inconsistent with his sense of honor, so he stayed to fight, facing the entire enemy fleet. The fight, which began in the afternoon, lasted through the night and into the next day; the English fleet had fled as night fell, leaving Grenville and the men of the *Revenge* to fight alone.

Half of Grenville's crew of about two hundred had been sick when the fight began; by morning the ship, which had received eight hundred heavy shot, resembled a "slaughterhouse." Grenville himself was dying of wounds in the chest and head. He commanded the master gunner to blow up and sink the ship; but the captain and master, not wanting to sacrifice the lives of everyone on board, intervened and arranged a surrender with the Spanish. Grenville, who is reported to have shown his defiance of death and his captors by chewing the wineglass they gave him until blood ran from his mouth, died as an honored guest aboard the enemy flagship.

The Spanish, who had lost hundreds of men in the fight, enjoyed their prize only a short time; the *Revenge* sank in a storm just after it was seized. Though Grenville's story has been held up ever since as an example of the unparalleled courage and sense of honor of the Elizabethans, it also illustrates how cheaply those from the upper ranks held the lives of men of the "meaner sort." Grenville was prepared to sacrifice all those who had not already been killed by destroying his ship; he reaped the glory, his men simply served. He died cursing those who had thwarted him in this final plan.

The sea war of the 1590s was costly in leaders. England also lost Sir Francis Drake and Sir John Hawkins in a singularly ill-planned venture to Panama in 1595. The faults of this expedition illustrate the conflict between the goals of making war against the king of Spain and seizing plunder. Usually, the two goals could be served simultaneously, but when they were in conflict chaos could result. Plunder frequently took priority, even in extreme circumstances. For example, Lord Charles Howard, overall commander of the English fleet facing the Armada, diverted his squadron in the decisive battle of Gravelines to loot a crippled Spanish ship that had run aground at Calais. Even official government action was supposed to produce its share of profits. After Drake attacked Cadiz in 1587 to cripple the intended Armada, he went on to the Azores to satisfy the merchants whose investment in the voyage had been for profit as well as patriotism. Capture of the carrack *San Felipe*, with a cargo worth £ 114,000, made the voyage a financial as well as a strategic success.

In the 1595 expedition, however, there was a conflict over aims, partly because of divided command. Hawkins and Drake, the joint commanders, did not see eye to eye. Their original goal was to capture and hold Panama, a reasonable aim since Panama was poorly defended and therefore vulnerable, and holding it would give England a base in the heart of the Spanish empire. By the time the expedition finally sailed at the very end of August, however, the plan had been changed to a hit-and-run raid on Panama, with stops to plunder along the way. Strategic considerations had been given up in favor of gaining loot. The new emphasis on plunder meant the voyage had very little chance of success, because the Spaniards already knew that Drake and Hawkins were preparing a major expedition; they were readying a fleet of their own, which left Spain shortly after the English sailed from Plymouth.

Time wasted in fruitless raids on the Canaries and Puerto Rico dissipated any chance of a surprise attack on Panama, and defenses there were bolstered by the time the English arrived. Hawkins, a sick man, had died in the Virgin Islands as the fleet prepared the attack on Puerto Rico. When it was repulsed, Drake took the fleet to the mainland and spent three weeks trying to extort plunder from a small pearl-fishing village. The mayor finally admitted that he had falsely claimed he was gathering the pearls demanded in order to gain time to warn settlements along the coast of Drake's approach. The attack on Panama was a disaster, partly because of poor information about the region. Drake took the fleet back to the islands, possibly hoping to find plunder there, but he was a broken man and the deadly climate began to take its toll, with fever and dysentery breaking out among the crew. Drake died of dysentery in January 1596. His lead coffin was cast into the sea to the sound of "doleful" trumpets. The entire expedition had been a disaster and a textbook illustration of the difficulties of conducting national policy through private enterprise.

Raleigh might have been among the great Elizabethans lost to the sea war of the 1590s. The *Revenge* was his ship and he had intended to command it on the 1591 expedition to the Azores until Queen Elizabeth intervened and forbade him. Raleigh was still one of her favorites, and she was not willing to risk his life. Once again, Grenville stepped in for his kinsman. Raleigh repaid the favor, turning Grenville's defeat into glorious triumph by writing a stirring account of the battle that inflamed English hearts.

Raleigh was the only one among the great Elizabethans who lived on long after the queen he loved had died, and his career veered between the highest peaks and the lowest valleys. In 1590, when the Roanoke colony was finally abandoned, Raleigh, though he was forced to share the charmed circle around the queen with Essex, was a rich and powerful man and becoming more so every day. The queen continued to add to his estates and sources of income; and he invested heavily in the sea war, amassing his own fleet of privateers. His intellectual interests were also growing and he attracted the best minds of the age to his London home, Durham House. He and his friends were involved in all aspects of the emerging new science, and they were not afraid to follow wherever their questions led them. He also began writing poetry more seriously now, and some of his poems indicated disenchantment with the artificial world of the court. Raleigh was a genuine Renaissance man, involved in all the serious intellectual currents of his time; his pride and arrogance were legendary. Among all his other interests, his American colony apparently just receded to the background.

Everything began to change in 1592. Raleigh, now almost forty, fell in love with one of Queen Elizabeth's ladies-in-waiting, Elizabeth Throckmorton, and they were married sometime during that year. The woman Raleigh chose gives another dimension to our understanding of his personality: she was as strong as he was. Bess Throckmorton was in her late twenties when they married and was not considered among the most eligible of the women at court. Raleigh chose character and intelligence over youth and beauty. Both of the Raleighs were going to need their strength in their lives together.

Queen Elizabeth hated to see those around her marry; she seemed to find the thought disgusting. Raleigh, as a favorite, was involved in constant playful pledging of undying love, a kind of mock courtship of the queen, who was soon to be sixty years old, so his secret marriage represented pure treachery in Elizabeth's eyes. When Bess Raleigh's pregnancy forced open avowal of the marriage, both husband and wife were arrested and confined in separate quarters in the Tower of London, a much more severe reaction than Raleigh had anticipated. Raleigh was briefly released to go to Dartmouth when the richest prize of the entire sea war, the *Madre de Dios*, was brought in by his privateers, but he was under guard the entire time. Raleigh's role was to try to stop the uncontrolled looting of the ship's cargo by everyone connected with the voyage, especially to make sure that Elizabeth and the government got their share; but he was returned to the Tower when the cargo was settled. The Raleighs were finally released in time for Christmas, but were exiled from court and sent to live in the country. Bess Raleigh was never again to be received at court.

For several years, Raleigh settled down to the role of country gentleman. He was especially active as a member of Parliament during this interlude. In 1593, the Raleighs' second son, Walter, called Wat, was born. The firstborn was not mentioned after his birth; he must have died, as did so many children in those days.

All during his period of exile, Raleigh was still spinning schemes designed to give England an overseas empire that would rival Spain's. Many people had pointed out that the territory of Guiana was virtually empty of European occupation and that it lay at the heart of the Spanish empire, a place that England might claim and colonize. Moreover, there were persistent rumors of vast wealth, goldmines, in Guiana, centered on the legendary golden city of Manoa in El Dorado. The idea of a vast treasure house was plausible because of the incredible wealth of the Incas and Aztecs that the Spanish had stumbled across in their early explorations. Moreover, the mines from which their gold came had never been found, so stories of mines deep in Guiana's jungle made sense. Their embellishment by tales of Indians who coated themselves with gold dust only whetted explorers' appetites. Raleigh had for some time been thinking of heading an expedition to Guiana and up the Orinoco River to find the mines, establishing an English claim to the territory at the same time. Now the idea began to dominate his thinking, because it was the kind of masterstroke that might restore him to the queen's favor.

Two years of campaigning finally won him a charter to explore, claim territories not already in the possession of any Christian king, and seize enemy trading vessels; but whereas the Roanoke patent had referred to him as "trusty" and "well-beloved," now he was simply "our servant Sir Walter Raleigh." A fleet of five ships was prepared, and many courtiers invested, some in person as well as financially. Lawrence Keymis, of Balliol College, Oxford, assumed the role of technical advisor that Hariot had earlier played. This was Raleigh's first voyage across the Atlantic, and much was riding on it. The expedition began well, as good relations were established with the natives of the region. The Indians were full of stories of bad treatment by the Spanish, and Raleigh was determined to make them love the English. Indian help was a cornerstone of his strategy.

From these beginnings, the venture quickly deteriorated because the English were not prepared for tropical conditions. The Orinoco is a spider's web of rivers, Raleigh called it a "labyrinth," and even the local Indians they obtained to guide them could not always find their way. Raleigh later wrote of the great beauty of the jungle and its birds and animals, but he also admitted that conditions were impossible. The heat and humidity were oppressive to Englishmen accustomed to a much milder climate, and the dense foliage hid countless terrors. In the end the explorers reported seeing jewels in the possession of Indians they had met along the way and brought back many samples of stones they believed to contain ores, but no solid proof of a mine, and much more convincing evidence that it would be difficult in the extreme for the English to hold that part of America.

Despite all the difficulties, Raleigh's account of the voyage, *The Discovery of the Large, Rich, and Beautiful Empire of Guiana*, was filled with hope for an English future there. It is interesting to compare Raleigh as a recorder with Hariot; they were the two most highly educated Englishmen to write about American experiences in the sixteenth century. Whereas Hariot had been careful to describe only what he himself had seen and verified, and reported the opinions of others very cautiously, Raleigh was seduced by the lush tropical environment into believing much more than he could testify to personally. He thought that stories from classical antiquity about men without heads whose eyes were in the middle of their chests or of the "very cruel and bloodthirsty" Amazons who consorted with men only during the month of April and only to gain female children were confirmed in the jungles of South America.

Though Raleigh never saw any of these human monsters, he always quoted someone whom he considered absolutely reliable who had. He was scornful of the Spanish governor of the region, whom he held captive for a while, because he was not interested in learning about the region. Raleigh, on the other hand, took every opportunity to add to his fund of knowledge, particularly by seeking out "all the aged men, & such as were greatest travelers." He wanted to know about the land, the rivers, and the inhabitants of the entire area, who warred with whom, and which tribes were allies. He pointed out to his Spanish counterpart that Cortéz and Pizarro had been victorious precisely because they were able to make use of divisions among the Indians they faced.

Raleigh's main concern in his book was to make sure that his failure to find a mine did not bring the entire enterprise into disrepute. Like Hariot, he was concerned to refute the slanders of his own men, who were evidently talking in the taverns and ridiculing the idea of a golden city. Raleigh wrote that he was not

> so far in love with that lodging, watching, care, peril, diseases, ill savors, bad fare, and many other mischiefs that accompany these voyages, as to woo my self again into any of them, were I not assured that the sun covereth not so much riches in any part of the earth.

He explained his lack of success by pointing to the fact that information about Guiana was so difficult to obtain, especially exact locations, and that misinformation had caused them to come at the wrong time of year, when the rivers were in flood.

Raleigh said that many of his men had picked up marcasite, which they mistook for gold, and brought it home. When they found it was not gold, they said there was no gold in Guiana and that they had been fooled. Raleigh claimed that he had deliberately kept his information from the men because he was afraid that if they knew the location of the mine, they might hire themselves out as guides to rivals, even from other countries, and undo all his careful planning. Therefore, he had not wanted to dig for gold until he was ready to begin full-scale workings. Nor did he want the Indians on whom he must rely to realize how important gold was to him for fear they would increase their demands in return for information and aid; for that reason he had fewer samples of genuine ore than he might have had. Despite his Roanoke experience, he claimed that he could have a colony in Guiana set up and completely self-sufficient in two years.

Raleigh clearly expected to be back in Guiana or to have his agents there very soon, and having trained interpreters who knew the country would make the next expedition that much easier. With that easy ability to dispose of the lives of the "lower orders" that was so characteristic of the Elizabethans, Raleigh left two boys behind in Guiana, Francis Sparrey and Hugh Goodwin, in return for the son of an Indian chief.

Sparrey was captured by the Spanish after some time and sent back to Europe; his story was later published by Samuel Purchas, Hakluyt's successor as chronicler of English voyages. Hugh Goodwin's story was more bizarre; he stayed in Guiana and was met by Raleigh when he returned more than twenty years later. By that time, he knew many Indian languages but had forgotten almost all his English. He was one lost colonist who was found again.

Did this experience of life in America make Raleigh think of his colonists farther north? In his description of the Guiana voyage, he claimed that he tried to call in at Roanoke, but contrary winds and the impatience of his men prevented him. Attempts to capture some Spanish treasure on the way home also failed. The trip was not a success, though Raleigh's account of the land and the voyage was widely read with great excitement. The queen was unmoved, and Raleigh remained exiled from the court.

Almost as soon as he returned from America, Raleigh was involved in another scheme that combined his two lifelong goals: obtaining gold and striking at the power of Spain. He joined with his erstwhile rival, the Earl of Essex, and the Lord High Admiral, Lord Charles Howard, in a plan to cripple Spain by sending an armada against it, an armada that would succeed where Spain's had failed. English planners felt bold enough to strike, not at Spain's empire, but at Spain itself. Whereas Elizabeth considered American schemes such as Raleigh's Guiana venture chimerical, an attack on Spain was a plan she considered workable and likely to bring in revenue by capturing some of the treasure fleet. She gladly gave her support to the idea. In the summer of 1596, a fleet of ninety-six English ships and twenty-four Dutch, with ten thousand soldiers aboard, sailed to attack Cadiz.

Raleigh took on the immense job of assembling men and supplies for the voyage. Recruitment of volunteers was augmented by the action of press gangs seizing men from villages all around London. His reward was command of one of the five squadrons into which the fleet was divided; his ship, the *Warspite*, was one of two brand-new vessels the queen had invested in the expedition. Raleigh was conspicuous in the action at Cadiz: as he forced his way into the harbor, he had his trumpeters blow a blast in answer to each volley from the Spanish shore batteries; and he and the other commanders wore their most colorful clothes in defiance of the snipers trying to pick them off. The English accomplished one of Raleigh's most cherished goals at Cadiz: they avenged Grenville and the *Revenge* by attacking the four apostle ships in the harbor. The *St. Matthew* and *St. Andrew* were captured. The *St. Philip*, the ship that had captured the *Revenge*, was blown up, as was the *St. Thomas*, after which the bay was said to have been filled with dead and dying Spaniards. Raleigh did not emerge unscathed from the fight. He was wounded by splinters driven into his leg when a cannonball struck the deck in front of him. The wound never healed properly, and he walked with a limp for the rest of his life.

As soon as the fighting was over, the English swarmed over Cadiz, taking possession of everything of value and seizing wealthy merchants to be held for ransom. Raleigh had himself carried ashore, but quickly returned to his ship because of his intense pain. He chafed at his inability to act, because he realized that a great Spanish merchant fleet with cargoes worth many times the plunder of Cadiz was sitting just a mile away on the other side of the harbor. The other commanders had reserved those ships to be dealt with later, but their delay was fatal. Philip II gave orders that the entire fleet was to be burned to prevent its falling into enemy hands. Spain was willing to accept a crippling sacrifice in goods and ships to cheapen the English victory. On the way home, the English sacked the city of Faro and seized its famous library for Oxford.

Elizabeth was displeased at the news that the merchant fleet had been lost, but her anger fell on the commanders of the expedition, Howard and Essex. Raleigh was restored to royal favor by Cadiz and was once again in constant attendance on Elizabeth in his role as Captain of the Queen's Guard, though Bess Raleigh was still not welcome at court. There were other, less successful, ventures in company with Essex, but the entente between the two men did not last. None of the ventures restored Raleigh's fortune. In 1597 he made a will that showed how his holdings had shrunk: only one of his privateering ships remained in his possession, and much of his land was gone. He had invested a fortune in the Guiana and Cadiz expeditions and had seen most of it swallowed up.

And the reign was coming to an end. Queen Elizabeth was now very old and in her last years. Prudent men were looking to the succession and seeking to cover themselves, which was something Raleigh would not do. Though Elizabeth refused to name her heir, most assumed, correctly, that it would be James VI of Scotland, who became James I of England, the first of the Stuart line of kings. For several years before Elizabeth's death in 1603, those closest to her had been in communication with James, soothing his fears about the succession and offering their support. Only Raleigh refused the overtures of Scottish agents. The queen did not know of the secret negotiations, nor did she know of Raleigh's loyalty. He lost a great deal and gained only honor by it. Some of those who corresponded with James warned him against elements hostile to him, and Raleigh was frequently named. Some writers actively worked to poison the future king's mind against him with fantastic allegations. The proud and arrogant Raleigh had many enemies, and their day was coming. When James first met Raleigh, he said to him, in the punning style he loved, "On my soul, man, I have heard rawly of thee."

Very shortly, Raleigh lost all his government sources of income and worse was to come because he was soon arrested and charged with treason. He found himself once again in the Tower. There were plots at the accession of James I, sponsored by Roman Catholic and pro-Spanish elements. A close friend of Raleigh's was involved in one of them, and Raleigh may have known or guessed some of the details, but that was the extent of his involvement. He admitted that he had been offered a retainer by the Spanish of £1500 per year, but had refused it. He was the last person to sacrifice the interests of England for the king of Spain, and he protested the "heavy burden of God, to be in danger of perishing for a prince which I have so long hated." Nonetheless, he was convicted of high treason in a trial scarcely worthy of the name in which the prosecution ranted and hectored him to cover their lack of evidence. There were few now to speak up for him; he had even been baited and attacked by crowds in the street on the way to the court. Only years later was it revealed that many of those around the king, Raleigh's chief accusers among them, did take annual payments from the king of Spain in return for whatever information they saw fit to send him.

Public sentiment turned in Raleigh's favor and there was great revulsion against the judgment and especially the conduct of the trial. An observer said some of the jurors actually knelt before Raleigh and asked his forgiveness. Nonetheless, the verdict stood, and Raleigh was condemned to the special death reserved for traitors:

That you shall be had from hence to the place whence you came, there to
remain until the day of execution; and from thence you shall be drawn
upon a hurdle through the open streets to the place of execution, there
to be hanged and cut down alive, and your body shall be opened, your
heart and bowels plucked out, and your privy members cut off, and
thrown into the fire before your eyes; then your head to be stricken off
from your body, and your body shall be divided into four quarters, to be
disposed of at the king's pleasure: And God have mercy upon your soul.

Raleigh was not executed, nor were others of the convicted conspira-
tors. James I dangled the prospect of execution before them until the
last minute and then sent reprieves. Raleigh was condemned to remain
a prisoner in the Tower for the rest of his life; he actually lived there
for twelve years. In many ways, his imprisonment was not difficult to
bear. Though he could not leave the Tower, his friends and relatives
could visit him there, and he had sumptuous apartments to receive
them in. Bess Raleigh and Wat lived much of the time with Raleigh
in the Tower. The Raleighs' son Carew was born in the winter of
1604–1605. Raleigh threw himself into his studies, particularly of science and medicine. He set up a small laboratory and a garden in which
to grow medicinal herbs, including exotic ones that his various ventures had brought back. One of his friends from the earlier intellectual
circle at Durham House, the Earl of Northumberland, was sent to the
Tower in 1605 because of a vague supposed connection with the Gunpowder Plot of that year. Thomas Hariot came frequently; and a minia-
ture scientific society was set up, with the three men and their aides
working on various experiments.

Raleigh became famous as a medical man, and fashionable people
flocked to his prison to get his "cordials." One of these was Queen
Anne herself, the wife of James I. She began to visit Raleigh regularly
and brought her son Prince Henry, the Prince of Wales, with her.
Prince Henry was about fourteen when the visits began. He had
unbounded admiration for Raleigh and little for his father. From a
young age, the Prince of Wales customarily was maintained in a
separate establishment from his family, and his household became a
magnet for those who were dissatisfied with the reigning monarch.
This happened to an extraordinary degree in Henry's case. All those in
England who were dissatisfied with James and his policies looked to the
sensitive and intelligent Henry for future salvation, and Raleigh was

chief among them. Henry is reputed to have said that only his father would keep such a bird in a cage.

Because Henry was so eager to learn from him, Raleigh began to write again, and a steady stream of papers on all aspects of government came from his pen. In Henry's interest, Raleigh began his most monumental work, the *History of the World*, in which he showed that God controls history and uses his power to punish unworthy monarchs, especially those who become tyrannical. Though James I suppressed it for a time, the *History of the World* was a best-seller, going through ten editions in the century, and was a major influence on those who came after him. Raleigh stopped writing and England's hopes were disappointed, though, when Prince Henry died at the age of eighteen. He was an athletic young man, who insisted on swimming in the foul Thames, where he apparently caught the typhoid fever that killed him. At the end, Queen Anne insisted that the doctors send to Raleigh for his "Great Cordial," but, though Henry rallied after taking it, he was dead the same day. The incident exposed the sham of Raleigh's position: if he had really been a traitor, no one would have allowed him to administer drugs to the heir to the throne.

King James was out of sympathy with the country, especially in his foreign policy. He had replaced the militant anti-Spanish stance of Elizabeth with a profound commitment to pacifism and friendship with Spain, a policy he hoped to crown with the marriage of the new Prince of Wales, Charles, to a Spanish princess. The sea war was ended as soon as he was established on the throne, and his major goal henceforth was to avoid war at all costs. Though most of his subjects remained anti-Spanish and strongly Protestant in outlook, James surrounded himself with pro-Spanish courtiers and allowed great latitude to the Roman Catholic gentry. One of his closest advisors was actually the Spanish ambassador, the future Count of Gondomar. James was comfortable with this policy, and he may have recognized that France was again becoming a power under the reintegrating reigns of Henry IV and Louis XIII. Though no one realized that the great power of Spain was virtually at an end, far-seeing counselors could argue that maintenance of the balance of power might soon require accommodation with Spain against a resurgent France.

James especially wanted to keep the peace because war was the single most expensive enterprise in which a country could engage. The king was deeply in debt, and his indebtedness was growing by great leaps. This was partly because he and his family were extravagant, but also because England was in a period of very great inflation; the income that had been sufficient for Elizabeth was far from enough for James and his large family. Every time he needed money, he had to go to Parliament and ask for it, and they were apt to require concessions of him before they granted new taxes. In peacetime, he could keep his indebtedness short of disaster; if he were to become involved in war, he would lose his independence as king. So James forged a policy that most of his subjects thought of as weak and cowardly, a policy Raleigh may have been ridiculing in his *History* when he contrasted the great Queen Semiramis with the weak, effeminate Ninias who succeeded her in ancient Assyria.

Raleigh, for his part, dreamed of action while in the Tower. Throughout his imprisonment he campaigned to be allowed to return to Guiana in search of the gold he felt sure was there. He had had a part in sending out some expeditions there that, although they did not find an actual mine, heard talk of not just one but several rich sources of gold and silver. Raleigh argued that he had established an English claim along the Orinoco when the native chiefs had willingly given allegiance to England through him and had begged to be relieved of Spanish tyranny. Finally, in 1616, James ordered Raleigh released from the Tower to begin preparations for a major expedition to Guiana that sailed in 1618.

The Walter Raleigh who wandered around a changed London in 1616 was far from the great knight of Elizabeth's reign. He was now over sixty and had had two strokes in the Tower, which, combined with the effect of the leg wound at Cadiz, gave him a shrunken appearance. Nonetheless he set out with great zest to plan for the voyage that could recoup all his fortunes. It was to be an expedition on the scale of the great Elizabethan ventures. He assembled a fleet of fourteen ships, but he sadly said the sailors were the "scum of the earth" and the masters were untrustworthy. Everything the Raleighs had left went into the preparations; Bess even sold her own remaining property. This was to be a make-or-break proposition.

King James made sure that Raleigh's future was indeed riding on his adventure in Guiana. The king let him go, lured on by the prospect of wealth so great that it could give him the independence of Parliament he craved. In doing so, he tacitly endorsed Raleigh's argument that England had a claim in Guiana; otherwise he was underwriting an invasion. On the other hand, he forced Raleigh to accept impossible conditions: there should be no clash with any Spanish subjects that would lead to loss of Spanish lives. Raleigh was convinced that he could head for the mine without going near the small Spanish settlement at San Thomé and gambled that, even if the Spanish tried to stop his men from digging and removing gold, the king would not punish him for resisting as long as he brought back a sufficiently rich cargo. Surely even James would be willing to fight to maintain an English presence in a territory that included a good mine.

Preparations for the expedition could hardly be concealed from Gondomar, so James took steps to conciliate the Spanish ambassador in advance. He demanded that Raleigh give him a complete itinerary of the intended voyage and a description of all the ships in the fleet including their armaments. These he handed over to Gondomar, who forwarded them to Spain. Raleigh and his men were shocked to find an exact copy in the hands of the Spanish governor in Guiana, though it had arrived too late for him to plan in any significant way. James also secretly promised Gondomar that, if Spanish lives were lost by action of Raleigh's men, Raleigh and his commanders would be handed over to Spain to be hanged in the market square in Madrid. He would not be dragged into an unintended war.

Once in the tropics, Raleigh was gratified to find that his name and reputation for fair dealing were still known among the Indians. Soon, though, everything began to go wrong. Tropical fever, possibly malaria, raged through the crews and struck Raleigh himself. He was too weak to explore Guiana in person; so it was decided that Lawrence Keymis, his trusted technical advisor, and Wat Raleigh, then about twenty-two, would take five ships and four hundred men up the Orinoco. This exploration was confused in conception and execution, possibly because Keymis and Raleigh had been discussing two possible mines. Keymis made no real attempt to travel to the mine away from the Spanish settlement that he and Raleigh had agreed on as a destination and, largely through the hotheadedness of Wat Raleigh, the party attacked and took San Thomé. Wat was killed in the attack; and Keymis, who returned to the waiting fleet to report the debacle, committed suicide. Between them, they had ruined Raleigh, though he had brought ruin on himself by gambling so heavily on a goal that had never been more than a theoretical possibility. In fact, Guiana did have reserves of gold, but it took modern mining equipment to develop them.

Raleigh wanted to sail to Newfoundland, restore the health of his men, and then return, refitted and revictualed, to Guiana to try again, but the men mutinied. Even before Keymis' return to confront Raleigh, the ships had begun to disappear one by one. Some went privateering on their own; others sailed back to England. Raleigh made for Britain; he never seriously considered escaping to France, where a friendly welcome awaited him, because his friends had put up a large bond for his return, and he would not disappoint them. When, later, he did try to escape it was too late.

James decided to hold a hearing in private; he was not willing to risk Raleigh's turning the crowd in his favor as he had done at his trial in 1603. Before the panel even assembled to hear his case, the execution warrant had already been signed on the basis of his conviction fifteen years before, despite many appeals for mercy, even from Queen Anne herself. Though he was still shaking with tropical fever, Raleigh conducted himself with exceptional presence at his hearing and execution. The king, over the horrified objections of his Privy Council, offered to make good on his promise to let Philip III carry out the sentence, but the Spanish monarch wisely allowed James to do his own dirty work.

Raleigh was executed the morning after his hearing, the sentence having been commuted from the hanging, drawing, and quartering of the original to death by beheading. Those who witnessed it never forgot the impression it made on them. Raleigh's execution scene is one of the most famous in history. He had apparently been in despair after his return to London as a prisoner, and he had become disheveled in appearance. Once it was clear he would be executed, though, a cloud seemed to lift from him. Knowing his fate gave him renewed strength. He became his old self again and actually took control of his own execution. Those around him were amazed at his self-possession; he was even cheerful as he greeted old friends. He gave a long speech from the scaffold explaining his conduct, and then asked to see the axe. When the reluctant executioner showed it to him, he said, in a now-famous simile, "This is a sharp medicine, but it is a sure cure for all diseases." He told the axeman that he would signal him when to strike and he refused a blindfold—he would be in control up to the end. He answered his friends who suggested he should face east toward Jerusalem, "So the heart be right, it is no matter which way the head lieth." Like his contemporary, William Shakespeare, Raleigh was a man who helped shape the way the English language is used.

It was ironic that Raleigh, who had been condemned on the ridiculous charge of favoring the interests of the king of Spain, should now be executed for having attacked Spanish claims. In his death he became a hero of the English people, who saw him as having died fighting for the country's true interests. All the resentment of his former wealth and arrogance evaporated, and he became an important symbol to those who opposed the Stuarts and their goals, particularly the pro-Spanish foreign policy. Raleigh, now seen as a victim of tyranny, was championed; his works were reprinted by those who led the country into civil war two decades later, a conflict that ended in the execution of Charles I, the son of James and younger brother of Henry, in 1649. They saw Raleigh as the original promoter of a great English nation leading the cause of Protestantism and carrying English trade and culture to the rest of the world. In this sense Raleigh was a bridge from the age of Elizabeth to that of the Puritan Lord Protector Oliver Cromwell, the first English ruler actively to sponsor colonization in the West Indies.[2]

From the 1590s on, Raleigh had been dogged by accusations that he was an atheist, a charge originally leveled by an English Jesuit propagandist, Father Robert Parsons, at the time of Raleigh's marriage and dismissal from the court. Calling one's opponent an atheist in those ideologically charged times was a tactic similar to a charge of communism in some quarters today. It might mean nothing more than that the victim was different or suspect in some way, especially when the indictment originated with a Jesuit who thought all Protestants had turned their backs on true religion. Since Parsons also called Lord Treasurer Burghley, Elizabeth's most trusted advisor, an atheist his accusations, though widely circulated, were completely suspect.

Some of the other accusations were similarly flawed. In 1593, Raleigh and some of his friends at a dinner party near his country home enjoyed the sport of running logical rings around a pompous parson; but their conversation was reported to the authorities and the result was the impaneling of a formal enquiry. Charges of impiety were taken very seriously. Suspicion of atheism followed Raleigh throughout his life and was used very effectively by Robert Cecil and Henry Howard, the two men who poisoned the mind of the future James I against him. The prosecution used Raleigh's reputation for atheism with deadly effect at his treason trial in 1603. So, deserved or not, the popular belief that Raleigh and his circle were skeptics in religion worked very great harm in the end.

Virtually every accusation included the name of Thomas Hariot, usually with the implication that it was Hariot who had led his master into impiety. All reports indicate that Hariot was much beloved of his friends and pupils, who included poets and playwrights as well as scientists. Why should such a mild person have a reputation so sinister? The answer seems to lie in his science, a study poorly understood in his day. The dividing line between science and magic was unclear even to scientists. Alchemy, for instance, was considered an important part of science, being practiced even by the great Isaac Newton at the end of the seventeenth century, and medical practice had a great many magical elements.

Because the scientist, like the magician, sought control over nature through special knowledge, it was difficult for early modern people to distinguish the two. Magic was considered dangerous, because the magician appropriated great power to himself, which could be used for good or evil. Virtually everyone believed in such power in Hariot's lifetime. Therefore a scientist was seen as one who dabbled in the "Black Arts," potentially able to bring great harm to the community. In 1605, at the time of the Gunpowder Plot, Hariot was briefly imprisoned because James I had heard rumors that he had cast horoscopes for the king and his children, something capable of the most evil interpretation. It was entirely believable to a man like the king that a scientist would create horoscopes in order to bewitch people.

Science was a suspicious calling for more fundamental reasons; it involved being willing to question all truths, test all dogmas. Science was potentially revolutionary because it elevated the individual's experience through experiment and observation over the word of authority. There is considerable evidence that Hariot was, according to his own lights, a religious man. His writings reveal that he thought of God as the all-important first cause, the creator of the natural order.

All human activities, or second causes, occurred, then, by God's permission within the universe he ordained.

Hariot, like many scientists since, thought of his work as explaining the principles of God's universe and its operation. Nonetheless, the disturbing problem remained: what if one's discoveries indicated truths that disagreed with those of the theologians? That was the situation in which empiricism became potentially dangerous. For example, the church taught that the heavens were perfect, that all forms within them were ideal geometric shapes. When Hariot built one of the earliest telescopes and began to study the skies systematically, he discovered, through his observation of Halley's Comet, that the orbits of heavenly bodies were elliptical, not perfectly round as theology demanded. He also studied the sunspots that marred the perfection of the sun's surface, and concluded that the sun was subject to decay and alteration just as the earth was. The implications of his findings were too revolutionary for his times.

There is considerable evidence from his papers, many only recently rediscovered, that Hariot's name should stand in the first rank of Renaissance scientists, along with such men as Galileo and Kepler. That it does not stems from the fact that he published almost nothing and left his papers in such a state that little was done with them after his death. Therefore, only a few knew of his work on the refraction of light through different substances, his contributions to algebraic theory and mathematical navigation, and his pioneering work on the telescope and the hundreds of celestial observations he made with it. The government's intolerance may have been partly responsible for England's loss of the glory Hariot's work should have brought. In a correspondence with Kepler, which Kepler initiated, Hariot reported on much of his work, particularly with refraction of light. He told Kepler that "our situation is such that I still may not philosophize freely; we are still stuck in the mud." Though his former pupil and friend Sir William Lower pointed out to him that others were getting credit for the breakthroughs he had made because of his "too great reservedness," Hariot published nothing of his scientific work. Perhaps the accusation of atheism had made him too cautious.

There is a further reason why Hariot even more than other Renaissance scientists might have followed intellectual pathways that carried him away from orthodoxy, one that grows out of his experience in America. Hariot took responsibility for discussing religion with the Indians, and his *Brief and True Report* makes clear that he thought deeply about that experience. On the one hand, his description of Indian religion forced him to acknowledge that there are universal elements in religion. Even though the natives' beliefs were generated without the benefit of divine revelation, they contained some echoes of true religion. Moreover, glad as he was of his success in communicating Christianity to the Indians, he was clearly disturbed by the fact that the Indians were interested in it because of English power and the technological marvels Hariot demonstrated for them, not because of its evident truth:

> Most things they saw with us, as Mathematical instruments, sea compasses, the virtue of the lodestone in drawing iron, a perspective glass whereby was shewed many strange sights, burning glasses, wild-fire works, guns, books, writing and reading, spring clocks that seem to go of themselves, and many other things that we had, were so strange unto them, and so far exceeded their capacities to comprehend the reason and means how they should be made and done, that they thought they were rather the works of gods then of men, or at the leastwise they had been given and taught us of the gods.

Hariot perceived that it was possible to manipulate people through their religious beliefs. He held the position of a prophet with the Indians, bringing a new and better religion; but he saw that, since they wanted Christianity in order to share English power, he could have offered them any set of beliefs and told them it was true religion. He believed the Indian priests controlled their people through their monopoly of the culture's theology; could the same thing happen in other cultures? Hariot must have talked about his speculations after his return from Roanoke. His incautious conversation may have been the source of a government spy's report that the poet and playwright Christopher Marlowe had been heard to say in a tavern that "Moses was but a juggler and that one Heriots being Sir W. Ralegh's man can do more than he," meaning that Moses had manipulated the religious beliefs of the Hebrews as Hariot had done with the Carolina Algonquians. Marlowe, who wrote *Doctor Faustus*, a play that describes a scholar who sold his soul to the devil in return for great knowledge, died soon after under a cloud of accusations. By all appearances, Hariot was chastened by both the spy's report and the fate of his friend. He became a cautious man.

Hariot and Raleigh remained associates throughout Raleigh's life. Hariot spent some time in Ireland, probably managing one of the Raleigh estates there. Once back in England, he acted for Raleigh in several capacities, managing most of his affairs while he was in Guiana in 1595. During the 1590s Hariot began to receive an annual pension from Raleigh's friend, the Earl of Northumberland, and he moved to Syon House, the earl's residence near London; but he always continued to work for and with Raleigh as well.

Northumberland's relationship to Hariot was different from Raleigh's; for him, Hariot was less a valued servant and more a fellow scientist. Northumberland gave him his own house on the grounds of Syon; and he had a library, observatory, and laboratory there with his own servants. Hariot was encouraged to follow his intellectual pursuits wherever they led, and he attracted pupils from all over the country. When the earl and Raleigh were in the Tower, where Northumberland stayed until 1621, the year of Hariot's death, Hariot functioned as their contact with the outside world, bringing books and papers and advising them on their experimental work. So close was their relationship that Raleigh may have asked Hariot to write out the notes he carried for his speech from the scaffold at his execution. A crumpled sheet in Hariot's handwriting listing the subjects Raleigh covered was found among Hariot's papers.

Despite their close association, there appears to be a great gulf between the outlook of Raleigh and that of Hariot. Raleigh is the last of the Elizabethans, interested in science but gripped by dreams of gold and swashbuckling exploits. Hariot, on the other hand, seems to be thoroughly modern; his outlook is completely experimental. He looks forward, whereas Raleigh forces our thoughts back to the Elizabethan age.

The cancer that killed Hariot grew slowly over many years, and was seen by some as God's judgment against him for his impiety. His will and his last few days reveal something about the man. He moved into London, possibly to be near his doctor, and spent his final days at the home of Thomas Buckner, a small merchant who had been one of Lane's colonists with Hariot. Apparently, the two men had developed a bond through that shared experience that remained strong for the rest of their lives. Hariot's will made bequests to all his servants and friends, acknowledged his debts, and showed him to be a careful, kindly man.[3]

Much less is known of the later lives of other actors in the Roanoke ventures. Ralph Lane, who was knighted in 1593, died in Ireland in 1603. A John White, "late of parts beyond the seas," died sometime before 1606, when his will was proved. He, like Lane, apparently died in Ireland. The courts had already decided that his daughter and her family were dead. In 1594, seven years after they had been left at Roanoke, a relative filed suit on behalf of Ananias' young son, John, to have his father declared dead. Eleanor Dare was apparently not John's mother, and the boy had been left behind in England. In 1597, he was granted his father's estate; in the eyes of the English courts, the colony had ceased to exist.

Most of those associated with the Roanoke colony were dead by the time the Elizabethan age ended. All they knew of English ventures in America were the successes of the privateers and the abject failure of everything else. They had no hint of the great British Empire that was to come. Only Thomas Hariot and Sir Walter Raleigh lived to see an English presence firmly established on the American coast, and they must have regarded the massive support the nation gave to Jamestown with a mixture of pride and chagrin. Jamestown's ultimate success was the result of a long, hard-fought campaign, with more setbacks and struggles than anyone would have anticipated. Hariot and Raleigh must have reflected bitterly on the fact that Roanoke, given the same level of commitment, would have been a glorious success.

10

EPILOGUE: THE NATURE OF SUCCESSFUL COLONIZATION

THOUGH Raleigh seems to belong to a far different era from that of Jamestown, the first successful English colony in America, he lived long enough to see it established and beginning to pay its way. His exclusive patent for colonization of North America had lapsed with his conviction for treason in 1603, and he had no right to object to the new colony when it was founded four years later, but he must have been incredulous that its promoters never sought the benefit of his experience. No one from the Virginia Company called on him for advice. Nor was Thomas Hariot consulted. Hariot's combination of scientific training and experience in the field should have made his help invaluable; but the company consulted him only once, two years after the colony's founding, when they asked him for a memorandum on native uses of copper. Virginia promoters apparently preferred to consult this controversial man through his book, the *Brief and True Report of the New Found Land of Virginia,* which they bought for the company's library. Richard Hakluyt was an investor and was involved in drawing up the company's initial instructions to the colonists. He apparently even considered going to the colony himself but decided that at fifty-four he was too old.

How much did Jamestown's planners learn from Roanoke's experience? The answer to that question is mixed. Some mistakes were avoided, but too many were made again and were corrected only after bitter experience. The first and most important lesson was that colonies require massive support over an extended period of time before they can stand on their own. The Virginia Company began, like

Raleigh's ventures, as a combination of merchants and gentry, but on a much larger scale. When the colony ran into trouble after the first two years, the company was reorganized and a clever device was used that vastly increased its base. Low-cost shares were sold throughout the country so that all property holders, not just great merchants and aristocrats, could invest. Everyone who was anyone became an investor. Since King James' pacific policy forbade any kind of open attack, all those who continued to aspire to a great international role for England and vengeance against Spain poured their energies and resources into the new colony. There was no privateering to divert their attention and men like John Watts, for example, were very active in the Virginia Company.

The Virginia Company was reorganized in 1609, a turning point that demonstrated how vastly England's situation had changed in the twenty years since the Roanoke colonists had been abandoned. Though the fleet taking the first settlers to Jamestown had been smaller than Grenville's, and the colony had been in serious trouble throughout its two-year existence, the company's reorganization made an enormous new effort possible. A great propaganda campaign was waged to attract investors: books, pamphlets, and sermons urged support of the colony as a patriotic duty. All investors were promised grants of land, one hundred acres for each share held, when the company was broken up after seven years. Those without possessions could adventure their persons; every colonist became a shareholder. Eventually further support was attracted to the effort as the company issued patents for "particular plantations" to groups of investors who could then govern and populate these landgrants for their own enrichment.

England was now prepared to support an American colony as a major goal in its own right. All the country's frustrations over the unsatisfactory peace with Spain went into supporting the colony, and some saw it as a future stronghold from which privateers could venture if the war should be resumed. Despite the fact that most shareholders never saw any return on their investments, money continued to flow into the colony. This consistent support made it a success where Roanoke had been a failure.

Jamestown's promoters selected Chesapeake Bay for its location; they clearly had studied Ralph Lane's descriptions of the area and its features. They set out to correct the greatest mistake made by the earlier colony; but in doing so, the colonists made some new errors of their own. They were told to look for a deepwater port, defensible against both the Indians and the Spanish. Hakluyt's notes of instruction for the new colony acknowledged that the Indians would inevitably resent the English intrusion on them, and he and the colonists were aware of the warlike reputation of the Chesapeake Bay Indians. Jamestown's site, on an island in the James River, was away from the coast and yet on a deep river that could accommodate ocean-going ships, excellent both for defense and for resupply. In choosing it, though, the governor and council had ignored Hakluyt's admonition to examine a prospective location for healthfulness. Jamestown, situated in a swampy area, was terribly unhealthy; the mortality rate among the colonists was enormous. Whereas the Roanoke colonists had been exceptionally robust under Lane, Jamestown's death toll in the first year reduced the original population from 105 to 38.

Some of Roanoke's lessons were obviously learned well, but too many others were ignored because they flew in the face of fundamental assumptions. The colonists chosen echoed Lane's company—a military organization staffed by young gentlemen, frequently younger sons looking for adventure and advancement, and soldiers, veterans of the Irish and European campaigns. Gentlemen, sometimes little more than boys, were put over experienced soldiers as in Roanoke purely because of their social status. The gentlemen, present in extraordinarily large numbers, did not expect to do manual work; nor did the servants with whom they surrounded themselves. The soldiers were hard to control and, as in Ireland, sometimes deserted to live with the surrounding natives. Since everyone there was in the employ of the company, there was little incentive to work hard. The Virginia Company experimented with government by a council that elected its president, but found that Lane's severe discipline worked better.

Jamestown's problems were far worse than Roanoke's. After the first great wave of mortality, the reorganized company sent a massive number of new settlers who confronted another wave of deaths. In a period of only six months the population was reduced from five hundred to sixty. There was a dramatic scene reminiscent of the Lane colony's decision to go home with Drake just before the first of the supply ships was about to arrive. The enfeebled Jamestown colonists decided to abandon the settlement in 1610 and were just leaving the mouth of the river when supply ships arrived, carrying a new governor and another large group of pioneers. Luckily, the men had been prevented at the last minute from burning the fort to the ground, and the colony went on. Despite its horrifying problems, the breaks were in Jamestown's favor, whereas they had always gone against Roanoke.

The Virginia colony's relations with the neighboring Indians were worse than those of Lane's men. Their swaggering military attitude alienated Indians already primed to resent the intrusion. Each side was dealing with a population that had experience of the other, and Hakluyt warned the colonists in their initial *Instructions* that the Indians would not "like your neighborhood." Despite the clear lesson of Lane's colony, the Jamestown settlers found themselves cajoling or extorting food from the Indians and, like Lane, accusing them of making war by withdrawing. Since the Powhatan Confederacy, in whose midst the colony settled, was highly organized, retribution could come more swiftly and effectively than on the Outer Banks. Though Powhatan's daughter, Pocahontas, a young tomboy who became the pet of the settlement, built some bridges between her father and the colony, Indian warfare punctuated its early years and sometimes kept the colonists virtually imprisoned within their stockade. Once Pocahontas reached puberty, her father sent her away from all contact with Jamestown, and warfare intensified.

The Virginia colony ultimately came to see what Raleigh had learned earlier, that a colony made up exclusively of young men of military background could not succeed. Only the presence of wives and children would make the settlers work hard to produce their own subsistence rather than trying to live as parasites on the Indians. This realization involved the further recognition that a colony must be a separate society; people must go to it expecting to stay and live out their lives there. If settlers saw service in America as a military role and expected to be rotated home in a few years, the commitment necessary to make the colony succeed would be lacking. The company sent shiploads of "maids" to be wives for the men already there and began encouraging families to emigrate. Young women and men, who indentured themselves to be servants for a number of years, usually seven, in order to pay their passage over, were promised land when their terms were up. They were to be the yeomanry of the new society.

The Virginia Company's emulation of the City of Raleigh model involved much more than just a different type of organization. Implicit in that decision was a recognition that the colony was not going to produce easily gained treasure. The soldiers sent in the earliest expeditions were told to search for gold and a passage to the South Sea; Captain John Smith, who thought all along that the search was in vain, fumed that time was wasted as the boats were loaded with "gilded dirt" while the crucial work of establishing the settlement was ignored. Now the company realized that the colonists would not be able to extort gold or other precious commodities from the Indians as the Spanish had done; nor could mines, if they existed, be discovered and developed until a thriving plantation had been founded.

The military model had been tried and had failed. The new plan, an attempt to recreate English society overseas, meant that the vision of Hariot and the Hakluyts was finally being put into effect. It was to be commodities produced by the colonists that would enrich the company and the country. Rocky times continued even after the Virginia Company began encouraging a family-centered colony; and it was a long time before tobacco, the commodity that was to bring success, was developed into a salable product. During the difficult early days when the colonists were struggling to stay alive and could not respond to the company's incessant demands to send home valuable commodities, John Smith said the directors in London had threatened simply to abandon the colony if it continued to be nothing but a drain on their resources. The shades of the lost colonists of Roanoke must have been on the minds of everyone in Jamestown. What had happened once could happen again. Jamestown was never abandoned, but many colonists were lost there because of the continuing high death rate. Of the six thousand sent to America by the Virginia Company, only about twelve hundred were alive in 1625. Jamestown's promoters were clearly willing to pour the "lower orders" into the venture regardless of their fate, just as promoters of Roanoke and of privateering had in the Elizabethan period.

John Smith is the pre-eminent symbol of Jamestown, as Raleigh is of Roanoke, and the two men could not be more different. Raleigh was the archetype of the swashbuckling aristocrat, searching for gain and glory together. His first colonists, greedily devouring rumors of pearls while hoping to construct a base for privateers, fitted that conception.

There was to be no grubbing in the soil for them. When Raleigh did finally send a colony designed to cultivate and develop American commodities, he lacked the resources and the interest to sustain it.

As Jamestown slowly slid into the successful family-centered model and sought to develop a genuine society of cultivators in America, the swashbuckling imagery dropped away. John Smith knew from the beginning that this would have to happen. He was unique among early English colonizers: a man chosen for command because of his skills rather than his social status. He shared Raleigh's arrogance, but its source was quite different. Smith was a self-made man. His father had been a yeoman farmer, substantial enough to buy his son an apprenticeship with a merchant but well below gentry status. His son, as a bright lad, had attracted the interest of the local lord of the manor, who had provided a grammar school education for him. Young John stayed in his boring apprenticeship only six months and then left to seek adventure in the European wars. His education henceforth was to be wholly practical. He consciously contrasted his experience with useless bookish learning when he said that he went first to "that university of war," the Low Countries. Then he set off for the frontier of Europe, where Islam and Christianity were locked in combat. By the time he was back in England in his early twenties, Smith had traveled throughout Europe and North Africa and had lived through almost incredible adventures. He had been knighted on the field of battle in Transylvania and had escaped from slavery in Turkey. The Virginia Company recognized that sending someone with Smith's experience of survival in alien lands would enhance the colony's chances of success.

John Smith never let anyone in Virginia forget that he was a survival expert, and he never troubled to conceal his contempt for the tender young gentlemen who did not know how to save themselves. He told the Virginia Company that a hundred "good laborers and mechanical men" would have accomplished more than "a thousand of those that went." Smith was hated by his fellow councilors; he finally became president by default when the others were all dead or incapacitated by sickness. When Smith was in command, everyone did manual labor, even the gentlemen, and deaths declined to a very small number. He felt he had proven conclusively that in the colonies skill, experience, and the capacity for hard work should count more than social status. Everyone there would have to contribute; no one could be purely ornamental. Smith personally exemplified a frightening specter to planners in London: the self-made man who could not be co-opted.

John Smith was as scornful of Virginia Company goals in the early years as he was of many of the colonists. Sudden wealth was not going to be Virginia's path to success; even if gold or a way to the Pacific were discovered, there would have to be a thriving colony to make use of them. He argued that first priority must go to establishing a viable settlement. Smith had independently arrived at a position similar to that of Hakluyt and Hariot. He pointed to Holland, quickly becoming one of the richest nations in Europe, and relished the fact that its wealth came from "that contemptible trade of fish." Smith was one of the earliest to recognize that all Spain's New World treasure had left that country more bankrupt than before. Trade in humble commodities was the path of the future.

To the extent that thoughtful readers looked beyond the boastful, argumentative tone of Smith's books and pondered the kernel of what he had to say, they must have found it deeply disturbing. Smith, in his vision of the British Empire, was describing a society in which the merchants, not the gentry, would dominate the economy. The Virginia Company was a continuation of the familiar model, a cooperative venture of the gentry, with their connections at court, and merchants, with financial and shipping resources; but Smith foresaw a future in which the merchants would be pre-eminent. Colonization and trade would ultimately transform English society.

Perhaps the Virginia Company was right after all not to consult Raleigh. His concept of colonization, despite the fact that he had been a leader in his alliances with the great Elizabethan merchants, was quaintly obsolete in the new century. When he was released from the Tower to pursue his anachronistic dream of gold in Guiana, the attention of the city was not on him, but on Pocahontas, newly arrived from Virginia and creating a sensation wherever she went. An expedition from Jamestown had found Pocahontas where she had been sent by her father and had kidnapped her and taken her back to the fort. There she was converted to Christianity and married to John Rolfe. She was the mother of an infant son when she arrived in London. Pocahontas died just as the ship that was to take her back to Virginia set sail. She was about twenty-one, a lost colonist of another sort. Other, more important, signs of the future were becoming evident. By 1618 when

Raleigh left on his last voyage, tobacco was becoming a boom crop in Jamestown. Commodities were already beginning to rule in place of gold.

England's new place in the world owed much to Roanoke and the sea war the colony had been designed to aid. The changes evident in the Virginia Company and its thinking would not have been possible without that earlier experience. Roanoke had contributed practical lessons, some of which were heeded, but the sea war, parasitic as it was, had also been important. The treasure that had been diverted into England from Spain provided much of the fluid capital now available for the new colony. England had a body of experienced men; gone was the dependence of English seamen on foreign navigators. Britain's mariners could now take their places with any in the world. Sailors of the seventeenth century were at home in the Atlantic as those before the 1580s had been in the English Channel. During the two decades of war against Spain, the foundations of England's greatness at sea were laid.[1]

Roanoke did not fade completely from English memories even after other colonies absorbed the nation's attention. There were many visitors to the region, beginning with John Pory of Virginia in 1622. One hundred years after the colony's disappearance, John Lawson of Carolina saw an artillery piece lying by the abandoned site. Seventeenth-century promoters sometimes analyzed Roanoke's failure, usually to imply that such a thing was no longer possible. But the specter of desertion with which the Virginia Company threatened its colonists always loomed as a possibility until the new settlements were well established and making their own way economically. A Newfoundland promoter, Richard Whitbourne, testified to the reality of this fear when he promised that colonists there would not be "left desolate in a remote Country."

Roanoke's story was retold in full in Robert Beverley's *History and Present State of Virginia,* published at the beginning of the eighteenth century. There are other echoes of the first colony in the seventeenth-century promotional literature, which make clear how English self-perceptions had changed. Raleigh's kinsman, Sir Ferdinando Gorges, attempted to found an empire in New England. In his call for colonists, he said how much better it was for English men to found a new nation than "servilely to be hired but as Slaughterers in the quarrels of Strangers." The former paths to glory, such as service in foreign wars, were now disdained, and colonization had become nation-building.

Despite the completeness of its failure and the depth of the tragedy, Roanoke has an important place in the foundations of the first British Empire and the beginning of the American nation. Whether any physical descendants of those several parties of lost colonists exist today, all Americans must trace their roots back to them. Their endeavor provided the experience to make later colonies succeed. Their failures and successes helped shape the ideology of colonization. The settlement and the sea war it was intended to serve provided the knowledge, and the means, for later victories; England was able to make good its claim to North America in the face of Spanish hostility, and the massive early failures at Jamestown, because of capital and experience gained between 1585 and 1604.

Roanoke is a fitting beginning for American history because it sets the theme of interdependence of the races that is the keynote of our history. Without Indian aid, there would have been no English colony in the seventeenth century. No early settlers, in New England or the South, were able to cope with their environment without crucial guidance and support from the Americans around them. The Indians also learned from English colonial ventures, and frequently the lessons were bitter ones. In the face of European arrogance, Indians showed a remarkable ability to borrow selectively from the alien culture while protecting the integrity of their own way of life. Only when the swiftly growing European-American populations robbed them of their farming and hunting territories did the Indians' culture begin to erode. The Indian contribution to the series of adaptations that formed American culture was crucial.

Actually, as throughout American history, there may have been three races in Roanoke. If, as we think, Drake did leave a sizable party of freed African slaves there when he picked up Lane's colonists in 1586, the major themes of American history were present from the very beginnings. The Indians, whose custom was to judge people by their usefulness rather than their color, would have adopted Africans and abandoned English colonists with equal enthusiasm. Unfortunately, though many aspects of Indian culture were borrowed and adapted by the invading Europeans, this openness about questions of race was seen as an oddity. The interdependence of the races continues as a theme right through our history, but the terms of the relationship very quickly ceased to be equal. Once English settlers were established here in sufficiently large numbers, they extended to the Indians and Blacks around them their notion that the "meaner sort" existed only to serve the interests of their betters. The races continued to be interdependent, but exploitation was the keynote of the relationship.

Roanoke exerts a pull on the late twentieth century because, however remote they seem, those involved in its story are identifiable to us as fellow human beings whose concerns we can recognize and sympathize with. Raleigh, White, and Hariot are intriguing partly because of the peculiar blend of the modern and the archaic they represent. At times their concerns seem wholly similar to ours—the scientific interest in America, for example. But, just when we are in danger of anachronistically erasing the four centuries that separate us, they take up positions that are profoundly remote from our concept of the normal.

More importantly, we can resonate to the Roanoke story because of its universal elements. Some aspects of the human situation do not change. Margaret Harvie and Eleanor Dare each giving birth to her first child in the roughest conditions, John White's anguish over his inability to return to his colonists, the mingled hopes and fears of the Indians as the English intruded with their attractive trade goods, Lawrence Keymis' despair and suicide, and Raleigh's resolution and cheerfulness at his execution—all these strike chords of understanding. Though almost all the social and political assumptions of both the Indians and the Elizabethans were different from ours, something about the starkness of their situation strips away the differences that separate us and reveals our common humanity. The Roanoke colonists actually seem closer to us than more recent but less understandable figures in our history, perhaps because later, more successful actors were better able to dominate their situations, to impose their own conceptions on the world around them, thus accentuating their distance from us. We can empathize with Raleigh's colonists and the Carolina Algonquians in the choices they had to make and the hardships they faced. Roanoke's enduring contributions—the lessons that made Jamestown and the later colonies possible, and the incomparable portraits of Indian culture produced by Hariot and White—make it truly the foundation of American history.

NOTES

Chapter 1   (pages 1–14)

1. This discussion follows closely on Wallace MacCaffrey, *Queen Elizabeth and the Making of Policy, 1572–1588* (Princeton, 1981). Those who want a full picture of the intricacies of English foreign policy in the 1570s and 1580s should read this excellent book.

2. For a full discussion of privateering in this period, see Kenneth R. Andrews, *Elizabethan Privateering: English Privateering During the Spanish War, 1585–1603* (Cambridge, 1964).

3. There are many biographies of Raleigh. Particularly helpful and interesting are Robert Lacey, *Sir Walter Ralegh* (London, 1973); Willard M. Wallace, *Sir Walter Raleigh* (Princeton, 1959); and David B. Quinn, *Raleigh and the British Empire* (New York, 1949).

Chapter 2   (pages 15–27)

1. On the career of Simon Fernandes, see David B. Quinn, "A Portuguese Pilot in the English Service," in his *England and the Discovery of America, 1481–1620* (London, 1974), 242–263. Fernandes' protestantism may have served to cover a Jewish identity. That would explain his hatred of Spain, which extended the Inquisition to Portugal after the union of the two kingdoms in 1580. See Henry W. Meyers, "The Jews in Tudor England and Their Presence on the Raleigh Voyages," paper delivered to the Southern Historical Association, Charleston, November 11, 1983.

2. On the life of Grenville, see A. L. Rowse, *Sir Richard Grenville of the Revenge: An Elizabethan Hero* (London, 1937).

3. On the historical geography of Roanoke Island, see Bruce S. Cheeseman's Historical Research Report *Four Centuries and Roanoke Island: A Legacy of Geographical Change* (Raleigh, N. C., 1982), 2–4, 12–15, 20–22; and Gary S. Dunbar, *Historical Geography of the North Carolina Outer Banks* (Baton Rouge, Louisiana, 1958).

4. On late sixteenth- and early seventeenth-century house and village construction, see Cary Carson, Norman F. Barka, William M. Kelso, Garry Wheeler Stone, and Dell Upton, "Impermanent Architecture in the Southern American Colonies," *Wintherthur Portfolio: A Journal of American Material Culture*, 16 (1981), 135–196; Ivor Noel Hume, *Martin's Hundred* (New York, 1982), Chaps. 11–12. On the bricks discovered at Roanoke, see J. C. Harrington, "Manufacture and Use of Bricks at the Raleigh Settlement on Roanoke Island," *North Carolina Historical Review*, 44 (1967), 1–17.

5. Anyone interested in the colony should visit Fort Raleigh National Historic Site, see the reconstruction, and talk with the exceptionally knowledgeable staff. I have especially benefited from conversation with Phillip Evans of Fort Raleigh and John Ehrenhard of the Park Service's Southeastern Archaeological Center. For a sampling of the theories about the colony's location, see J. C. Harrington, *Search for the Cittie of Raleigh: Archeological Excavations at Fort Raleigh National Historic Site, North Carolina,* Archeological Research Series Number Six, National Park Service, Department of the Interior (Washington, D.C., 1962) and *An Outwork at Fort Raleigh: Further Archaeological Excavations at Fort Raleigh National Historic Site, North Carolina* (Philadelphia, 1966); Cheeseman, *Four Centuries and Roanoke Island,* 19, 29–33; Phillip Evans, "Notes on the Location of the 'Cittie of Ralegh,' " unpub. ms. (Fort Raleigh National Historic Site, July, 1981); and David Durant, *Ralegh's Lost Colony* (New York, 1981), Appendix 2.

Chapter 3   (pages 28–44)

1. For further discussion of the life and work of these remarkable cousins and their writings, see E. G. R. Taylor, ed., *The Writings and Correspondence of the Two Richard Hakluyts,* 2 vols. (London, 1935). The work of the younger Richard Hakluyt is assessed in D. B. Quinn, ed., *The Hakluyt Handbook,* 2 vols. (London, 1974).

2. Yaupon *(Ilex vomitoria Ait.)* is a native tea high in caffeine used throughout the Southeast for ceremonial purposes. In high doses, it can induce vomiting as part of a purification rite. See Charles Hudson, *The Southeastern Indians* (Knoxville, Tenn., 1976), 226–228.

3. For further information about climate and vegetation on Roanoke, see Dunbar, *Historical Geography of the North Carolina Outer Banks,* Chaps. 1–2; and Cheeseman, *Four Centuries and Roanoke Island,* 6–7, 20.

4. For a full description of English society and its relationships, see Keith Wrightson, *English Society, 1580–1680* (London, 1982).

5. On Hariot, see John W. Shirley, ed., *Thomas Harriot, Renaissance Scientist* (Oxford, 1974).

6. Paul Hulton and David B. Quinn, eds., *The American Drawings of John White, 1577–1590,* 2 vols. (London and Chapel Hill, 1964).

Chapter 4   (pages 45–65)

1. I have benefited greatly from discussion with David Sutton Phelps of East Carolina University, who is writing the volume on the Carolina Algonquians for the Roanoke Quadricentennial Committee. On the culture of the Carolina Algonquians, see the article by William Sturtevant in Hulton and Quinn, *The American Drawings of John White,* I, 37–43; Christian F. Feest, "North Carolina Algonquians," in *Handbook of North American Indians,* William C. Sturtevant, Gen. Ed., XV, *Northeast,* ed. Bruce G. Trigger (Washington, D.C., 1978), 271–281; Hudson, *Southeastern Indians,* esp. chaps. 3, 4, and 6; and J. Frederick Fausz, *The Powhattan Uprising of 1622: "A Historical Study of Ethnocentrism and Cultural Conflict,"* unpub. Ph.D. diss., College of William and Mary, 1977.

2. Keith Thomas, *Religion and the Decline of Magic: Studies in Popular Beliefs in Six-teenth and Seventeenth-Century England* (Harmondsworth, England, 1973).

Chapter 5 (pages 66–87)

1. See Nicholas Canny, *The Elizabethan Conquest of Ireland: A Pattern Established, 1565–1576* (New York, 1976); and "The Permissive Frontier: Social Control in English Settlements in Ireland and Virginia, 1550–1650," in K. R. Andrews, N. P. Canny, and P. E. H. Hair, *The Westward Enterprise: English Activities in Ireland, the Atlantic, and America, 1480–1650* (Liverpool, 1978), 17–44.

2. The pearls were probably from fresh water mussels. Hariot later said the English had run across a few in eating mussels, but none of good quality. The 1585 colony was able to gather a large quantity of good pearls from the Indians.

Chapter 6 (pages 88–105)

1. Jamestown, founded in 1607, had a very high mortality rate from disease, which colonists attempted to blame on laziness and moral decay. See Karen Ordahl Kupper-man, "Apathy and Death in Early Jamestown," *Journal of American History*, 66 (1979), 24–40.

Chapter 7 (pages 106–121)

1. William S. Powell has found out as much as we know about the backgrounds of the Roanoke colonists. See his "Roanoke Colonists and Explorers: An Attempt at Identification," *North Carolina Historical Review*, 34 (1957), 202–226.

2. On life at sea in the sixteenth century, see Samuel Eliot Morison, "English Ships and Seamen, 1490–1600," in his *The European Discovery of America: The Northern Voyages, A.D. 500–1600* (New York,1971), 112–156; Kenneth R. Andrews, "The Eliza-bethan Seaman," *The Mariner's Mirror*, 68 (1982), 245–262; J. Watt, E. J. Freeman, and W. F. Bynum, eds., *Starving Sailors: The Influence of Nutrition upon Naval and Mar-itime History* (London, 1981); and Abbot E. Smith, *Colonists in Bondage: White Servitude and Convict Labor in America, 1607–1776* (Chapel Hill, 1947), Chapter 10. My knowledge of ship construction and shipboard life has been enhanced by discussion with Dr. Lokey Collins, historian at the Elizabeth II State Historic Site on Roanoke.

3. Simon Fernandes already had a reputation as a greedy and boastful man obsessed with privateering. See Elizabeth Story Donno, *An Elizabethan in 1582: The Diary of Richard Madox, Fellow of All Souls* (London, 1976), 147–148, 192.

Chapter 8 (pages 122–140)

1. Two excellent books tell the Armada's story in highly readable form: David Howarth, *The Voyage of the Armada: The Spanish Story* (New York, 1981); and Garrett Mattingly, *The Armada* (Boston, 1959).

2. Powhatan is best known to Americans as the father of Pocahontas. He was an ambitious state-builder; having inherited the overlordship of about six tribes from his father, he now controlled about thirty. The Chesapeakes were one tribe that had resisted his domination.

3. David B. Quinn, "The Lost Colony in Myth and Reality, 1586–1625," in his *England and the Discovery of America,* 432–481.

Chapter 9   (pages 141–163)

   1. See Karen I. Blu, *The Lumbee Problem: The Making of an American Indian People* (Cambridge, 1980), Chapter 2.
   2. On the life and work of Raleigh see, in addition to the biographies noted in Chapter I, V. T. Harlow, *Ralegh's Last Voyage* (London, 1932); Stephen J. Greenblatt, *Sir Walter Ralegh: The Renaissance Man and His Roles* (New Haven, 1973); Christopher Hill, "Ralegh–Science, History and Politics," in his *The Intellectual Origins of the English Revolution* (Oxford, 1965), 131–224. On the fiscal crisis confronting James I, see Conrad Russell, *The Crisis of Parliaments: English History, 1509–1660* (Oxford, 1971), 260, 272–281.
   3. For Hariot's life and career, see the essays in *Thomas Harriot, Renaissance Scientist,* ed. Shirley; and Henry Stevens, *Thomas Hariot: The Mathematician, the Philosopher, and the Scholar* (1900; rept. New York, 1972). On the question of Raleigh's and Hariot's atheism see, in addition to these, Stephen J. Greenblatt, "Invisible Bullets: Renaissance Authority and Its Subversion," *Glyph: Johns Hopkins Textual Studies,* 8 (1981), 40–61; Pierre Lefranc, *Sir Walter Ralegh, Ecrivain: L'oeuvre et les Idées* (Paris, 1968), Chap. 13; Ernest A. Strathmann, *Sir Walter Ralegh: A Study in Elizabethan Skepticism* (New York, 1951); and Jean Jacquot, "Thomas Harriot's Reputation for Impiety," *Notes and Records of the Royal Society,* 9 (1952), 164–187.

Chapter 10   (pages 164–173)

   1. Andrews, *Elizabethan Privateering,* Chapter 9.

INDEX